Cooking Up U.S. History

Cooking Up U.S. History

Recipes and Research to Share with Children

Second Edition

Suzanne I. Barchers
and
Patricia C. Marden

Illustrated by
Leann Mullineaux

1999
Teacher Ideas Press
Libraries Unlimited
A Division of Greenwood Publishing Group, Inc.
Westport, Connecticut

TEACHER IDEAS PRESS
Libraries Unlimited
A Division of Greenwood Publishing Group, Inc.
88 Post Road West
Westport, CT 06881
1-800-225-5800
www.lu.com/tip

Library of Congress Cataloging-in-Publication Data

Barchers, Suzanne I.
    Cooking up U.S. history : recipes and research to share with children / Suzanne I. Barchers and Patricia C. Marden ; illustrated by Leann Mullineaux. -- 2nd ed.
        xv, 203 p. 22x28 cm.
    Includes bibliographical references and index.
    ISBN 1-56308-682-4 (softbound)
    1. Cookery, American. 2. United States--History--Study and teaching (Elementary)   I. Marden, Patricia C., 1948-
II. Title.
TX652.B3155   1999
641.5973--dc21   98-55921
                                                                          CIP

Dedicated to Dan, Jeff, and Josh, who were always there.
S.I.B.

Dedicated to my family and friends
who all told me not to work too hard and who cared.
P.C.M.

Contents

Chapter 2: THE COLONIAL PERIOD (continued)

Chapter 3: THE REVOLUTIONARY WAR 37

Chapter 4: WESTWARD EXPANSION 51

Introduction

America has a rich heritage of cooking, beginning with the varied diet of the Native American Indians before the discovery voyages of the Europeans. Cooking in the classroom is an ideal way to enhance the study of American history in the elementary or middle school program. Cooking can be an occasional treat or a routine component of instruction. Teachers may use a cooking experience as an integral part of a thematic unit, to culminate a unit, or to observe a holiday. Students benefit from learning basic cooking terms and skills and from the cooperative preparation and consumption of new and different foods.

This second edition of *Cooking Up U.S. History* is an updated and enhanced compilation of recipes, research, and readings linked to the history of the United States. It not only provides teachers with classroom-tested recipes but also offers them in the context of the most commonly encountered social studies units: Native American Indians, the colonists, the Revolutionary War, the westward expansion, the Civil War, and the commonly identified geographic regions of the United States. Favorite recipes from the first edition have been retained, with new recipes added for variety. All chapters include updated bibliographies of related fiction, nonfiction, film, video, and CD-ROM for additional study. A separate bibliography devoted to books on food is also included. Helpful information on cooking terminology and measurement is supplied in the glossary and appendixes.

Recipe Selection

Recipes have been carefully researched and selected to reflect the practices of the period. However, because modern appliances such as mixers and ovens will be used, many recipes are modernized. Library Links may direct students to discover earlier methods of cooking.

The chapter on the colonists includes recipes for soap, candles, and ink. Though not for consumption, these items are included to illustrate how early settlers had to prepare a variety of necessities.

The number of servings given for each recipe generally indicates normal servings, such as one might have at home. They do provide enough for a "tasting party." Many recipes would have to be doubled or tripled to provide enough for a full meal for an entire classroom.

Some recipes accurately reflect the limitations of the food or resources of that time period. Therefore the foods may not be the most tasty or appealing. It is important for students to understand that for these recipes people often had to "make do." This is part of the adventure of cooking in the classroom!

Library Links

Each chapter includes a list of Library Links on a reproducible page that can be used as research or reference questions. The answers to some links can be found simply by consulting a dictionary. Some links are taken from books about food. (See the bibliography on page 175.) Some links require the use of encyclopedias, nonfiction books, or other reference materials. Answers to the Library Links are in appendix A, and they provide fascinating information about the historical period, food, and regions.

Introductions to the Chapters

The introductory page to each chapter provides an alphabetical listing of terms about the period or region. These ABCs can be used as vocabulary lessons or in trivia challenges.

Bibliographies

The bibliographies for chapters 1 through 5 (Native American Indians, The Colonial Period, The Revolutionary War, Westward Expansion, and The Civil War) provide many opportunities for further research or for the use of historical fiction. Bibliographies for the regional chapters do not include titles on specific states or cities. Consult your library for books to supplement your study. There are fewer historical fiction titles in the regional chapters; however, many titles found in chapters 1 through 5 also apply to the study of regions.

It is difficult to indicate reading levels, as the range of reading ability varies widely in a classroom. If the reading level is indicated as "grades 3 and up," it means that it could be read by the more advanced third grader and older children. A designation of "all ages" means that the book is a resource or a picture book that is worth using with all ages.

A Final Recommendation

Many of the recipes are simple and require little preparation. The new classroom cook should start with the less challenging recipes. For example, it is easy to bring an electric griddle into the classroom to make sourdough pancakes.

Other recipes are more demanding and require the use of a kitchen. Some schools are well equipped for such an undertaking. Some PTAs or student councils have funded a convection oven and a collection of cooking equipment that is stored on a cart for convenient sharing. Consider using an electric frying pan, toaster oven, or crock pot.

Read each recipe carefully to determine the demands of the preparation with the limitations of your classroom in mind. There is enough variety to meet numerous needs.

Cooking and Safety Tips

1. Read recipe carefully before beginning.

2. Make sure no one has a food allergy.

3. Gather all ingredients, utensils, bowls, and other equipment.

4. Turn on the oven to preheat, if needed.

5. Measure exactly.

6. Make sure you have completed each step before proceeding to the next one.

7. Time any baking or cooking carefully. All baking temperatures are indicated in Fahrenheit.

For Safety's Sake

1. An adult should help with oven or stove usage. Always use thick, dry potholders to handle hot equipment.

2. Turn off stove and oven when cooking and baking are completed.

3. If grease should catch fire, pour baking soda on the fire. Do not pour water over the flames. If the fire is in a pan, put the lid on to smother the flames.

4. Always tie back long or loose hair when working around the oven or stove. Be careful with loose sleeves or clothing.

5. Keep hands and face away from steam when cooking liquids over a stove.

6. When cooking with saucepans, always turn the handles so they don't stick out over the edge of the stove.

7. During cooking, allow as few people as possible around hot items. It is best to designate an adult to remain in that area.

8. Sharp instruments should remain on tables when not in use and should be carefully carried to a sink for cleanup by an adult.

9. When peeling vegetables, always move the blade away from your hands.

10. Use a cutting board to protect counter tops when cutting or chopping. Always cut away from your hands.

11. Wash knives and other sharp instruments separately from other tools and be careful when wiping the blades.

12. Make sure that your hands are dry whenever plugging in or using electrical appliances.

13. Do not immerse electrical appliances in water when cleaning them. Refer to manufacturer's directions for cleaning.

From *Cooking Up U.S. History*, Second Edition. © 1999 Suzanne I. Barchers and Patricia C. Marden. Teacher Ideas Press. (800) 237-6124.

1
Native American Indians

Native American Indians

Word List

- Acorn
- Biscuitroot
- Cranberry
- Dyes
- Elders
- Filbert
- Groundnut
- Hickory nut oil
- Ink berry
- Juneberry
- Kinnikinnick
- Leek
- Mayapple
- Nodding wild onion
- Ostrich fern
- Papaw
- Quills
- Rose hips
- Skunk cabbage
- Toothwort
- Utensils of birch bark
- Viburnums
- Wild rice
- X
- Zuni bread

From *Cooking Up U.S. History*, Second Edition. © 1999 Suzanne I. Barchers and Patricia C. Marden. Teacher Ideas Press. (800) 237-6124.

The Native American Indian Diet

When the first settlers arrived in America, the Native American Indians enjoyed an abundant and varied diet, drawing upon more than 2,000 different plant foods, plus nuts, fruit, fish, seafood, and available game. Their diets were limited only when nature intervened.

They were skilled farmers, adapting their methods to the earth and to the needs of the people. They steadily improved the cultivation of beans and corn.

It has been estimated that more than 65 percent of our contemporary diet can be traced directly to the contributions of Native American Indians. The single most important contribution, however, is corn.

Corn feeds the animals that produce:

meat
poultry
milk
cheese

Corn oil is found or used in the making or packaging of:

soap
insecticides
mayonnaise
salad dressings
monosodium glutamate

Corn syrup is found or used in the making of:

candy
ketchup
ice cream
processed meats
soft drinks
beer
gin
vodka
sweetened condensed milk

Corn starch is found in:

puddings
baby foods
jams
pickles
vinegar
yeast
instant coffee

powdered sugar
potato flakes
toothpaste
cosmetics
match heads
charcoal briquettes

Nuts

Native American Indians ate a wide variety of nuts, usually collected by the women and children. The nuts were prepared in many ways, and eaten raw as well. The following recipes may be used with any nuts that the Native American Indians ate: black walnuts, hickory nuts, hazelnuts, pecans, pine nuts, beech nuts, chestnuts, and acorns.

ROASTED NUTS

Ingredients
Nuts

Steps
1. Shell nuts.
2. Spread nuts in one layer on a cookie sheet.
3. Bake at 300 degrees, stirring often so they don't burn.
4. Bake for about 15 to 20 minutes or until nuts become somewhat crisp. Experiment with the baking time to achieve desired taste.

GRINDING NUTS

Ingredients
Nuts

Equipment
Nut grinder

Steps
1. Put a small amount of shelled nuts into nut grinder.
2. Grind nuts into a bowl. This process grates them into dry pieces and not an oily clump.

GROUND NUT CAKES

Ingredients
1 cup ground nuts   1 teaspoon vanilla
½ cup maple syrup   ½ cup flour

Steps
1. Mix nuts, syrup, and vanilla.
2. Stir in flour.
3. Form dough into 1-inch balls.
4. Place on greased cookie sheets.
5. Bake at 350 degrees for 5 to 10 minutes or until firm and browned.

Makes 15 to 20 cakes.

From *Cooking Up U.S. History*, Second Edition. © 1999 Suzanne I. Barchers and Patricia C. Marden. Teacher Ideas Press. (800) 237-6124.

NUT BUTTER

Ingredients
1 cup nuts
½ teaspoon salt

Steps
1. Grind nuts in a blender until pasty. Some nuts made need a bit of oil added.
2. Stir in salt.

Makes 1 cup.

ACORN MUSH

Ingredients
Acorns
Water

Steps
1. Shell nuts and dry them in the sun for three to five days.
2. Grind nut meats into flour by putting them through a meat grinder or blender.
3. Put acorn flour in a fine strainer.
4. Pour warm water over nut flour.
5. Continue pouring water over flour and increasing the temperature of the water until boiling water is used.
6. Continue pouring water over flour, tasting until flour is sweet instead of bitter.
7. Strain mush.
8. Refrigerate mush until it is used.

ACORN MUSH SOUP

Ingredients
1 quart acorn mush
1 gallon water
Salt

Steps
1. Simmer acorn mush and water until it is the desired thickness.
2. Add salt to taste.

Makes 2 or more quarts, depending on thickness of soup.

From *Cooking Up U.S. History*, Second Edition. © 1999 Suzanne I. Barchers and Patricia C. Marden. Teacher Ideas Press. (800) 237-6124.

PEMMICAN

Ingredients
1 pound dried beef or buffalo meat
⅔ cup raisins
Suet or lard

Steps
1. Cut dried beef into small chunks.
2. Put beef and raisins in a meat grinder and grind together.
3. Pat beef and raisin mixture into a shallow pan.
4. Melt suet.
5. Pour melted suet over top of mixture to cover.
6. Stir mixture together and allow it to cool.
7. Mixture may be cut into squares to eat.

Serves 4 to 6.

COOKED BEANS

Ingredients
4 cups dried beans (usually navy or pea beans)
Water
1 teaspoon baking soda
½ pound salt pork or ¼ pound bacon
½ cup molasses
2 small onions, chopped

Steps
1. Put beans in large pot and cover with water. Soak overnight.
2. Drain beans.
3. Cover beans with fresh water and bring to a boil. Simmer for 1 hour.
4. Drain beans. Add 6 cups of fresh water, baking soda, and the salt pork or bacon.
5. Simmer for 45 minutes.
6. Pour beans in a greased casserole dish with just enough of the liquid to cover them.
7. Add onions and molasses and stir well.
8. Bake in 350 degree oven for 3 to 4 hours or until tender. If beans start to dry out add more water.

Serves 8.

From *Cooking Up U.S. History*, Second Edition. © 1999 Suzanne I. Barchers and Patricia C. Marden. Teacher Ideas Press. (800) 237-6124.

HOMINY

Ingredients
1 quart dried whole ears of corn
Water
2 tablespoons baking soda
1 ¼ teaspoons salt
Butter

Steps
1. Wash corn with warm water.
2. Put corn in a stainless steel pan.
3. Add 2 quarts of water and baking soda.
4. Put a lid on the pan and let the mixture sit overnight.
5. Put pan on the stove and bring mixture to a boil.
6. Simmer for 3 hours.
7. Drain the corn and put into cold water.
8. Rub the corn until the hulls are removed.
9. Drain corn and put in saucepan again with 2 more quarts of cold water.
10. Bring to boil.
11. Simmer for 1 hour.
12. Drain, put in cold water, and rub hulls off again.
13. If hulls are not removed at this point, repeat boiling/rubbing process.
14. When hulls have been removed, drain and stir in salt and butter to taste.

Serves 4 to 6.

DRIED CORN

Ingredients
3 ears sweet corn

Steps
1. Cut corn kernels from the cobs.
2. Spread kernels one layer deep on cookie sheets.
3. Put cookie sheets in a 175 degree oven for several hours until kernels are dried.

Makes approximately 3 cups.

PARCHED CORN

Ingredients

3 tablespoons butter or margarine   Salt
3 cups dried corn (see recipe on page 7)

Steps
1. Melt butter in a large skillet.
2. Put one layer of corn kernels at a time in the skillet.
3. Heat over medium-high heat, stirring constantly.
4. Kernels are done when they turn brown and puff up (about 4 minutes).
5. Add salt to taste.
6. Repeat until all kernels are cooked.

Serves 4 to 6.

WILD RICE WITH BLUEBERRIES

Ingredients

1 cup wild rice   1 teaspoon salt
2 ½ cups water   1 cup blueberries

Steps
1. Wash and drain rice three times.
2. Put rice, water, and salt into a saucepan. Cook over low heat until water is absorbed and rice has softened (about 45 minutes).
3. Stir in blueberries.
4. Serve warm.

Serves 4 to 6.

CORN AND EGGS DISH

Ingredients

½ pound solid bacon   1 cup corn kernels
3 eggs

Steps
1. Cut bacon into 1-inch cubes.
2. Fry bacon in a skillet over medium-high heat until crisp and brown.
3. Pour off the liquid fat.
4. Reduce heat to low.
5. Beat eggs in bowl and stir in corn.
6. Pour egg mixture over bacon in skillet.
7. Stir and cook until eggs are done.

Serves 4.

From *Cooking Up U.S. History*, Second Edition. © 1999 Suzanne I. Barchers and Patricia C. Marden. Teacher Ideas Press. (800) 237-6124.

ZUNI SUCCOTASH

Ingredients
½ pound beef, cut into small squares
4 cups water
2 cans corn, drained
2 cans string beans, drained
1 cup sunflower seeds, shelled
Salt and pepper

Steps
1. Boil beef squares in water until tender.
2. Add corn and string beans and heat thoroughly.
3. Mash sunflower seeds by placing seeds between waxed paper and pressing with a rolling pin.
4. Bring beef mixture to a boil again and add mashed seeds, stirring well.
5. Simmer until broth has thickened.
6. Add salt and pepper to taste.

Serves 4 to 6.

CORN ROLLS

Ingredients
1 cup white cornmeal
1 cup yellow cornmeal
¾ teaspoon pepper
1 cup boiling water
½ cup melted fat (buffalo fat or bacon drippings)
Green corn husks

Steps
1. Mix together cornmeals and pepper.
2. Stir in water and fat.
3. Shape dough into small rolls.
4. Wrap individually in corn husks.
5. Put in a 9-x-13-inch pan.
6. Bake in a 350 degree oven for 1 hour.

Serves 5.

From *Cooking Up U.S. History*, Second Edition. © 1999 Suzanne I. Barchers and Patricia C. Marden. Teacher Ideas Press. (800) 237-6124.

FRY BREAD

Ingredients
3 cups flour
2 ½ teaspoons baking powder
1 teaspoon salt
2 tablespoons melted lard or shortening
2 cups water
Hot fat for frying

Steps
1. Mix flour, baking powder, and salt in a large bowl.
2. Stir in melted lard or shortening.
3. Pour in water a little at a time until mixture forms a soft dough. You may need to use more than 2 cups.
4. Knead dough a few times. Do not handle too much or dough will become tough.
5. Break off pieces of dough about the size of a small biscuit and flatten to ¼-inch thick.
6. Melt fat in a large skillet over medium-high heat.
7. Fry dough in fat until golden brown.

Serves 6.

BOILED SQUASH PUDDING

Ingredients
2 large acorn squash
3 apples
Water
½ cup maple syrup or maple sugar (brown sugar may be substituted)
½ teaspoon salt

Steps
1. Peel squash and cut into small chunks.
2. Put squash in saucepan and add water to about 1-inch deep.
3. Peel, core, and cut apples into chunks.
4. Add apples to squash.
5. Bring water to a boil.
6. Simmer over low heat until squash and apples are soft. Add water if needed.
7. Remove pan from stove.
8. Mash and stir squash and apples.
9. Add maple syrup and salt and stir thoroughly.
10. Serve warm or cold.

Serves 6 to 8.

POPCORN BALLS

Note: This was a special treat for the children during maple syrup boiling time.

Ingredients
¾ cup maple syrup
3 cups popped popcorn

Steps
1. Boil maple syrup in saucepan over medium heat until it reaches 250 degrees or the hard-ball stage, turning hard and crunchy when a drop is dropped into cold water.
2. Pour maple syrup over popcorn in a large bowl. Stir quickly.
3. When syrup cools enough to be handled, roll into balls.
4. Put balls on greased waxed paper until they cool completely.

Makes 5 to 6 medium-sized popcorn balls.

Library Links

Library Link 1:   What does *pawcohiccora* mean?

Library Link 2:   The peanut is an important American food. Find some products of the peanut used today.

Library Link 3:   How were acorns ground before grinders were available?

Library Link 4:   How was pemmican stored for carrying?

Library Link 5:   Find the earliest record of the existence of beans.

Library Link 6:   In what form was corn first found?

Library Link 7:   Where was the first evidence of corn found?

Library Link 8:   Where was wild rice found in North America?

Library Link 9:   Find several Native American Indian spellings of succotash.

Library Link 10:   Research the eating customs of the Native American Indians.

Library Link 11:   Research the agricultural skills of the Native American Indians.

Library Link 12:   How did the Native American Indians pop their popcorn?

Bibliography—Native American Indians

Nonfiction—Series

Glubock, Shirley. *The Art of the North American Indians.* New York: Harper and Row, varying dates. Grades 2 and up.

Photographs of Native American Indian masks, clothes, pottery, totems, and other museum artifacts demonstrate the range of Indian art. See also titles of the art of the Southwest, Northwest Coast, Plains, Woodlands, and Southeast Indians.

Porter, Frank W., editor. *Indians of North America.* New York: Chelsea House, varying dates. Grades 4 and up.

This extensive series provides colorful descriptions of the histories, lifestyles, customs, and challenges of many different tribes. Photographs, glossaries, and maps make these books especially useful.

Nonfiction—Individual Titles

Ashabranner, Brent. *A Strange and Distant Shore: Indians of the Great Plains in Exile.* New York: Dutton, 1996. Grades 4 and up.

In 1875 the U.S. Army forced several tribes onto reservations. This book is the story of 72 chiefs who were sent to an old Spanish fort in St. Augustine, Florida, as punishment for their raids against settlements.

Caduto, Michael J., and Joseph Bruchac. *Keepers of Life: Discovering Plants Through Native American Stories and Earth Activities for Children.* Golden, Colo.: Fulcrum, 1994. All ages.

As with *Keepers of the Earth,* this resource provides an abundance of activities that develop an understanding of plants, botany, environmental issues, and ecology. A teacher's guide is also available.

———. *Keepers of the Animals: Native American Stories and Wildlife Activities for Children.* Golden, Colo.: Fulcrum, 1991. All ages.

This extensive resource contains 27 animal stories and numerous related activities that promote understanding of and appreciation for animals. Activities include the arts, theater, reading, writing, science, social studies, mathematics, sensory awareness, and creative thinking. A teacher's guide is also available.

———. *Keepers of the Earth: Native American Stories and Environmental Activities for Children.* Golden, Colo.: Fulcrum, 1988, 1989. All ages.

The format of this book is similar to *Keepers of the Animals,* but it focuses on environmental activities. A teacher's guide is also available.

———. *Keepers of the Night: Native American Stories and Nocturnal Activities for Children.* Golden, Colo.: Fulcrum, 1994. All ages.

Contains a variety of activities related to the stories of the night.

———. *Native American Gardening: Stories, Projects and Recipes for Families.* Golden, Colo.: Fulcrum, 1996. All ages.

Provides related stories and information for "Three Sisters" gardening: growing squash, beans, and corn.

Echo-Hawk, Roger C., and Walter R. Echo-Hawk. *Battlefields and Burial Grounds: The Indian Struggle to Protect Ancestral Graves in the United States.* Minneapolis, Minn.: Lerner, 1994. Grades 4 and up.

Complete with fascinating photographs, maps, and drawings, this book explores the conflict between those who want to study Native American Indians through their grave sites and the descendants who want to preserve their spiritual practices.

Freedman, Russell. *An Indian Winter.* New York: Holiday House, 1992. Grades 4 and up.

Using the journal of Prince Alexander Philipp Maximilian and the paintings of Karl Bodmer, Freedman describes the life of two Europeans befriended by Native American Indians during a difficult winter.

Harvey, Karen D., and Lisa D. Harjo. *Indian Country: A History of Native People in America.* Golden, Colo.: Fulcrum, 1994. Teacher resource, grades 5 and up.

Lesson plans, essays, stories, poems, and speeches document the Native American Indians' history.

Hunter, Sally M. *Four Seasons of Corn: A Winnebago Tradition.* Photographs by Joe Allen. Minneapolis, Minn.: Lerner, 1997. Grades 3 and up.

Twelve-year-old Russell learns the history of the traditions of corn from his grandfather. Photographs and text intersperse the history with Russell's contemporary life.

Hunter, Sara Hoagland. *The Unbreakable Code.* Illustrated by Julia Miner. Flagstaff, Ariz.: Northland, 1996. Grades 3 and up.

When John's mother decides to marry and leave the reservation, he is concerned about leaving behind his traditions. His grandfather reminds him that he knows the unbreakable code, which was invented using the Navajo language during World War II.

Johnson, Sylvia A. *Tomatoes, Potatoes, Corn, and Beans: How the Foods of the Americas Changed Eating Around the World.* New York: Atheneum, 1997. Grades 5 and up.

Johnson describes how a variety of foods were used by the Native Americans, how they traveled to other parts of the world, and how their uses then changed. Featured foods include maize, beans, peppers, peanuts, potatoes, tomatoes, and chocolate. Includes line drawings, maps, and photographs.

Wolfson, Evelyn. *From Abenaki to Zuni: A Dictionary of Native American Tribes.* Illustrated by William Sauts Bock. New York: Walker, 1988. Grades 3 and up.

The locations, dwellings, food, clothing, and transportation are discussed for 68 North American Indian tribes. The maps, symbols, labeled drawings, glossary, and index provide an excellent research tool.

Fiction

Bierhorst, John. *The Woman Who Fell from the Sky.* Illustrated by Robert Andrew Parker. New York: Morrow, 1993. Grades kindergarten and up.
 In this Iroquois creation tale, a husband pushes his wife from the sky. She gives birth to two children, Sapling and Flint, whose differences explain the harsh winters.

Bruchac, Joseph. *The Boy Who Lived with the Bears and Other Iroquois Stories.* Illustrated by Murv Jacob. New York: HarperCollins, 1995. Grades 1 and up.
 This collection of stories emphasizes the relationship between humans and the natural world.

———. *Dog People: Native Dog Stories.* Illustrated by Murv Jacob. Golden, Colo.: Fulcrum, 1995. Grades 3 and up.
 These six stories celebrate the relationship between youngsters and dogs.

———. *The Great Ball Game: A Muskogee Story.* Illustrated by Susan L. Roth. New York: Dial, 1994. Grades kindergarten and up.
 In this Native American Indian legend the animals and birds play a ball game to settle an argument.

Bruchac, Joseph, and Gayle Ross. *The Story of the Milky Way: A Cherokee Tale.* Illustrated by Virginia A. Stroud. New York: Dial, 1995. Grades kindergarten and up.
 When a magic dog eats a tribe's food, a young boy and a wise woman work together to get rid of him. His trail creates the Milky Way.

Bruchac, Joseph, and James Bruchac. *Native American Games.* Golden, Colo.: Fulcrum, 1999. Grades kindergarten and up.
 Provides stories about and directions for a variety of Native American Indian games.

Bruchac, Joseph, and Jonathan London. *Thirteen Moons on Turtle's Back.* Illustrated by Thomas Locker. New York: Philomel Books, 1992. Grades 2 and up.
 Bruchac and London provide a Native American Indian poem for each of the moons found on the back of a turtle.

Bunting, Eve. *Cheyenne Again.* Illustrated by Irving Toddy. New York: Clarion, 1995. Grades 1 and up.
 When Young Bull is taken to a Native American Indian reservation school he resists attempts by teachers to change him. He tries to keep the Cheyenne inside him.

Goble, Paul. *Adopted by the Eagles: A Plains Story of Friendship and Treachery.* Scarsdale, N.Y.: Bradbury Press, 1994. Grades kindergarten and up.
 White Hawk and tall Bear, two Lakota friends, risk their friendship as they hunt for horses in enemy territory.

———. *Her Seven Brothers.* Scarsdale, N.Y.: Bradbury Press, 1988. Grades 3 and up.
 Goble uses stunning illustrations and lyrical prose to retell the Cheyenne Indian legend of the Big Dipper.

From *Cooking Up U.S. History*, Second Edition. © 1999 Suzanne I. Barchers and Patricia C. Marden. Teacher Ideas Press. (800) 237-6124.

———. *Iktomi and the Buzzard: A Plains Indian Story.* New York: Orchard, 1994. Grades kindergarten and up.
Iktomi the trickster plots to get across a river without getting wet.

———. *The Lost Children: The Boys Who Were Neglected.* New York: Maxwell Macmillan International, 1993. Grades kindergarten and up.
This legend tells of neglected boys who became the stars we call the Pleiades.

Greene, Ellin. *The Legend of the Cranberry: A Paleo-Indian Tale.* Illustrated by Brad Sneed. New York: Simon & Schuster, 1993. Grades kindergarten and up.
The Paleo-Indians used the mastodons as beasts of burden until they became untrustworthy and had to be destroyed.

Gregory, Kristiana. *Jenny of the Tetons.* San Diego, Calif.: Harcourt Brace Jovanovich, 1989. Grades 4 and up.
Carrie is wounded and alone after a Native American Indian attack. She is cared for by a trapper whose wife, Jenny, is a Shoshone Indian. Carrie begins to respect Jenny and the Indians' regard for the land.

Hausman, Gerald. *How Chipmunk Got Tiny Feet: Native American Animal Origin Stories.* Illustrated by Ashley Wolff. New York: HarperCollins, 1995. Grades kindergarten and up.
These seven Native American Indian tales are suitable for telling.

Hobbs, Will. *Bearstone.* New York: Atheneum, 1989. Grades 4 and up.
A young Ute, sent to work for an old rancher, struggles to control his anger and determine where he belongs. With the rancher's patience and through meeting a challenge, he discovers his internal powers.

Hotze, Sollace. *A Circle Unbroken.* New York: Clarion Books, 1988. Grades 4 and up.
Rachel was captured by Native American Indians in 1838 and was lovingly raised as the chief's daughter. When her father, a stern minister, recaptures her, she longs to return to the tribe.

Martin, Rafe. *The Rough-Face Girl.* Illustrated by David Shannon. New York: Putnam, 1992. Grades 2 and up.
In this Cinderella-like tale, the young girl is covered with scars. Her purity and strength of heart lead her to happiness with the Invisible Being.

McDermott, Gerald. *Coyote: A Trickster Tale from the American Southwest.* New York: Harcourt Brace, 1994. Grades kindergarten and up.
In this Zuni tale, Coyote wants to sing, dance, and fly like the crows.

———. *Raven: A Trickster Tale from the Pacific Northwest.* New York: Harcourt Brace, 1993. Grades kindergarten and up.
Raven describes how the sun was stolen from the Sky Chief and given to the humans in this Pacific Northwest tale.

Oughton, Jerrie. *The Magic Weaver of Rugs: A Tale of the Navajo.* Illustrated by Lisa Desimini. Boston: Houghton Mifflin, 1994. Grades kindergarten and up.
Spider Woman teaches two Navajo women the necessary skills for making rugs.

From *Cooking Up U.S. History*, Second Edition. © 1999 Suzanne I. Barchers and Patricia C. Marden. Teacher Ideas Press. (800) 237-6124.

Regguinti, Gordon. *The Sacred Harvest: Ojibway Wild Rice Gathering.* Minneapolis, Minn.: Lerner, 1992. Grades 2 and up.
Color photographs and text describe a young boy's first time gathering wild rice in northern Minnesota.

Taylor, Harriet Peck. *Coyote and the Laughing Butterflies.* New York: Macmillan, 1995. Grades kindergarten and up.
Coyote is tricked by some butterflies in this story of the Southwest. The butterflies laugh so hard they can no longer fly straight.

Thomas, Kenneth. *Naya Nuki: Shoshoni Girl Who Ran.* Illustrated by Eunice Hundley. Jackson, Wyo.: Grandview, 1991. Grades 4 and up.
Naya Nuki and her friend, Sacajawea, are captured by a rival tribe. Naya Nuki plots her escape. While running back to her Shoshone people, she encounters and triumphs over many dangers.

Van Laan, Nancy. *Buffalo Dance: A Blackfoot Legend.* Illustrated by Beatriz Vidal. Boston: Little, Brown and Company, 1993. Grades 1 and up.
This Blackfoot legend explains the ritual dance performed before and after a buffalo hunt.

———. *Shingebiss: An Ojibwe Legend.* Boston: Houghton Mifflin, 1997. All ages.
Despite the severe winter, a bird keeps alive by burning one log each month and finally tricking Winter Maker into leaving.

Whelan, Gloria. *The Indian School.* New York: HarperCollins, 1996. Grades 2 and up.
Lucy must live with her stern aunt and uncle who run a school for Native American Indian children. Through her friendship with two youngsters, she teaches her aunt and uncle compassion.

Young, Ed. *Moon Mother.* New York: HarperCollins, 1993. All ages.
This legend describes the separation of the spirit people from those on earth.

CD-ROMs

Native Americans 1. Washington, D.C.: National Geographic, 1995. Grades 4 and up.
Explores the major tribes of the eastern woodlands and Great Plains.

Native Americans 2. Washington, D.C.: National Geographic, 1995. Grades 4 and up.
Learn about the Native American Indians of the Southwest, Northwest Coast, and Arctic.

Video

American Indians: A Brief History. Washington, D.C.: National Geographic, 1985. 22 minutes. Grades 4 and up.
Provides an overview of the first Americans and the arrival of the white settlers and their impact on Native American Indians.

2
The Colonial Period

The Colonial Period

Word List

- Alewives
- Butter paddle
- Corn, cranberries
- Dutch oven
- Elk
- Flax
- Grist mill
- Ham
- Indian pudding
- Jerusalem artichoke
- Kettle
- Lug pole
- Mortar, maple sirup (syrup)
- Niddy noddy
- Onions
- Pestle
- Quern, quahog
- Roasting ears
- Salt saler (saltcellar)
- Trestle table
- Utensils
- Verjuice
- Wooden spoons
- X
- Yellow eyes
- Zenger, Peter

From *Cooking Up U.S. History*, Second Edition. © 1999 Suzanne I. Barchers and Patricia C. Marden. Teacher Ideas Press. (800) 237-6124.

PORRIDGE

The pilgrims often had porridge for breakfast, or oatmeal with breakfast. They served it with hasty pudding (see following recipe).

Ingredients
4 cups water
½ teaspoon salt
2 cups old-fashioned oats
Molasses or maple sugar

Steps
1. Pour water in saucepan and bring to a boil over medium-high heat.
2. Stir in salt and oats.
3. Turn heat down to medium. Cook and stir mixture for about 10 minutes.
4. Cover pan and remove from heat.
5. Let stand until thickened (5 to 10 minutes).
6. Serve with molasses or maple sugar.

Serves 6.

HASTY PUDDING

Hasty pudding, or cornmeal mush, was a staple of the early colonists' diet. They served hasty pudding warm with molasses poured over it for breakfast. For lunch and dinner they cooled and sliced it.

Ingredients
2 cups water
⅓ cup cornmeal
½ teaspoon salt
Molasses or maple syrup

Steps
1. Put water in the bottom and 2 cups water in the top of a double boiler and boil over medium heat.
2. Stir in cornmeal and salt.
3. Cook until thick, about 1 hour, stirring occasionally.
4. Serve warm with molasses or maple syrup, or cool and slice to eat.

Serves 4.

CORNMEAL PUDDING

Ingredients
4 ½ cups milk
⅓ cup cornmeal
½ cup molasses
¾ teaspoon salt

Steps
1. Heat the milk in a saucepan until it is scalded.
2. Place cornmeal in the top of a double boiler.
3. Slowly pour in the scalded milk, stirring constantly.
4. Cook the mixture in the double boiler over medium heat for 20 minutes.
5. Add molasses and salt and stir well.
6. Butter a baking dish.
7. Pour the cornmeal mixture into the baking dish.
8. Bake mixture in the oven at 325 degrees for 1 hour or until firm.

Serves 4 to 6.

JOHNNYCAKES OR JOURNEY CAKES

Ingredients
1 egg
2 cups cornmeal
¾ teaspoon salt
1 ½ cups milk
Butter
Powdered sugar, if desired

Steps
1. Beat egg.
2. Stir in cornmeal, salt, and milk.
3. Drop spoonfuls of batter on a well-greased, hot griddle.
4. Fry until brown on both sides.
5. Serve hot with butter and/or powdered sugar.

Makes 10 to 12.

CORN STICKS

Ingredients

1 ¼ cups milk
1 cup cornmeal
¾ cup flour
¾ teaspoon salt
3 teaspoons baking powder

⅓ cup molasses
2 eggs, beaten
2 tablespoons oil
2 tablespoons butter, melted

Steps

1. Heat milk in saucepan until it is scalded.
2. Put cornmeal in a mixing bowl and pour the hot milk over it.
3. Mix thoroughly and let it cool to lukewarm.
4. Add the flour, salt, and baking powder to the cooled cornmeal mixture and stir.
5. Stir in the molasses, beaten eggs, oil, and melted butter.
6. Pour the mixture into a well greased bread-stick pan.
7. Bake in the oven at 400 degrees for about 20 minutes.

Makes approximately 12 corn sticks.

OLE KOOKS

Ingredients

2 cups milk
1 cup butter
3 eggs, separated
1 ¼ cups sugar
1 package dry yeast
¼ cup warm water

3 ½ cups flour
¼ cup chopped raisins
½ teaspoon nutmeg
¼ cup milk
Hot fat for deep frying

Steps

1. Put milk in a small saucepan.
2. Add butter and warm over low heat until the butter gets soft. Set aside.
3. Put egg yolks into a small bowl. Beat well, adding sugar while beating. Continue beating until all sugar is mixed in.
4. In a small metal or glass bowl, beat egg whites until light peaks form.
5. In a large bowl, mix together yeast and warm water.
6. Stir milk, egg yolks, and egg whites into yeast mixture.
7. Add enough of the flour to make a soft dough. Add more if necessary. Knead to mix all ingredients.
8. Put dough back in the large bowl. Cover with a soft cloth.
9. Put dough in a warm place and let rise until double in size, several hours or overnight.
10. Soak raisins and nutmeg in ¼ cup milk for about 30 minutes.
11. Pour off milk and mix raisins and nutmeg into dough that has risen.
12. Prepare hot fat for frying by heating to 370 degrees.
13. Pinch off pieces of the dough about the size of an egg. Fry them in the hot fat 10 to 12 minutes until they puff up and brown.
14. Drain on paper towels.

Serves 10.

From *Cooking Up U.S. History*, Second Edition. © 1999 Suzanne I. Barchers and Patricia C. Marden. Teacher Ideas Press. (800) 237-6124.

BUTTER

Ingredients
Heavy whipping cream
Salt (to taste)

Steps
1. Take cream out of refrigerator for about an hour before making butter.
2. Pour cream into a glass jar that has a tight-fitting lid. Fill only half full.
3. Shake jar until curd (solid) separates completely from whey (liquid).
4. Pour whey into a separate container. This may be drunk as buttermilk.
5. Pour curd into a strainer and let drain for several minutes until all liquid is drained off.
6. Place curd into a bowl and stir in salt.
7. Use butter as desired.

BLACK BEAN SOUP

Ingredients
2 cups black beans
3 quarts water
1 ½ onions, sliced
3 bay leaves
3 stalks celery, chopped
½ pound salt pork
Salt and pepper (to taste)

Steps
1. Soak beans in the water overnight.
2. The next morning, add the rest of the ingredients and cook over low heat.
3. Cook until beans are soft and mushy, adding more water as needed.
4. Press entire bean mixture through a coarse sieve, pushing through all possible ingredients.
5. Add water, salt, and pepper as necessary.
6. Reheat mixture to serve.

Serves 4 to 6.

SQUASH SOUP

Ingredients
2 large squash
1 ½ cups boiling water
4 ½ cups milk
3 tablespoons butter
Salt and pepper (to taste)

Steps
1. Peel the squash, cut in half, remove the seeds, and cut into small pieces.
2. Cook the squash in boiling water until it is soft.
3. Scald the milk.
4. Mash the squash and then stir in the scalded milk.
5. Heat, but do not let mixture boil.
6. Stir in the butter, salt, and pepper.

Serves 4 to 6.

FISH CHOWDER

Ingredients
3 tablespoons shortening
1 onion, sliced thin
2 ½ pounds fresh fish (cod, haddock, etc.)
3 raw potatoes, peeled and chopped into small pieces
Water
2 tablespoons melted butter
2 tablespoons flour
3 cups milk
1 ½ teaspoons salt
¼ teaspoon pepper

Steps
1. Melt shortening in a large saucepan.
2. Cook onion in it until the onion is tender.
3. Remove skin and bones from the fish.
4. Cut fish into small pieces.
5. Add fish and potatoes to saucepan and cover with water.
6. Cover and cook over low heat until potatoes are tender.
7. Mix butter and flour in a bowl.
8. Add a little of the hot fish water to flour mixture and stir.
9. Pour flour mixture into broth and stir.
10. Add milk, salt, and pepper.
11. Stir and simmer for a few minutes.

Makes approximately 3 quarts.

SUCCOTASH

Ingredients
2 cups fresh lima beans
Water
3 ½ cups fresh corn kernels
5 tablespoons butter
Salt and pepper (to taste)

Steps
1. Place lima beans in boiling salted water.
2. Cover and cook about 30 minutes or until tender.
3. Add the corn and stir.
4. Pour off extra water so that remaining water just covers corn.
5. Cook over low heat about 5 to 10 minutes or until most of the water has evaporated.
6. Stir in butter, salt, and pepper.

Serves 6 to 8.

PILGRIM'S DESSERT (STEWED PUMPKIN)

Ingredients
Fresh pumpkin, peeled, seeded, and cut into cubes
Water
Ginger (one teaspoon for 1 medium saucepan of pumpkin)
Molasses (to taste)

Steps
1. Put pumpkin cubes in a saucepan.
2. Add water to about 1-inch deep in the pan.
3. Cover and cook over medium heat until pumpkin is soft and mushy. Stir occasionally.
4. Stir in ginger to taste.
5. Let pumpkin cool slightly and serve in bowls with molasses on it.

Serves 4 to 6, depending on size of pumpkin.

BROWN BETTY

Ingredients
8 slices toast
½ cup sugar
1 teaspoon cinnamon
¼ cup butter
6 apples, peeled and sliced
½ cup molasses
⅔ cup water
Whipped cream, optional

Steps
1. Crumble all of the toast.
2. Sprinkle one layer of toast crumbs (about half of them) in the bottom of a 9-by-13-inch baking pan.
3. Sprinkle with half of the sugar and half of the cinnamon.
4. Use half of the butter and dab it all over the crumb mixture.
5. Layer half the sliced apples over the mixture.
6. Sprinkle the rest of the toast, sugar, cinnamon, butter, and apples over the first layer.
7. Mix water and molasses and pour over entire mixture.
8. Set baking pan in a larger pan that contains 1 inch of hot water.
9. Bake at 400 degrees for 40 to 50 minutes.
10. May be served with whipped cream for a more modern version.

Serves 6 to 8.

BERRY INK

Ingredients
⅔ cup ripe fresh or frozen berries (blueberries, strawberries, raspberries, etc.)
½ teaspoon salt
½ teaspoon vinegar

Steps
1. Fill a strainer with berries and place it over a bowl.
2. Use a large spoon and crush the berries, letting the juice strain into the bowl.
3. Keep adding berries to the strainer until all berries have been crushed.
4. Throw the berry pulp away.
5. Add the salt and vinegar to the berry juice and stir.
6. Store berry ink in a jar with a lid.

From *Cooking Up U.S. History*, Second Edition. © 1999 Suzanne I. Barchers and Patricia C. Marden. Teacher Ideas Press. (800) 237-6124.

NUT INK

Ingredients

6 whole walnut shells   ½ teaspoon vinegar
¾ cup water   ½ teaspoon salt

Steps

1. Crush the empty shells by wrapping them in a towel and smashing them with a hammer.
2. Put the crushed shells in a pan and add the water.
3. Put the pan on the stove and bring the water to a boil.
4. Turn the heat down and let the water simmer for about 45 minutes, until it turns dark brown.
5. Let the mixture cool. Pour it through a strainer into a jar.
6. Add the vinegar and salt to the ink.
7. Use nut ink with quill or wooden pens.

HAND SOAP

Caution: Lye use requires adult supervision. Lye flakes are poisonous and burn skin. If lye touches skin, immediately flood area with water. Do *not* use an aluminum pan. Soap making may produce smoke and irritating fumes.

Ingredients

32 ounces olive oil   6 ounces lye flakes
14 ounces vegetable shortening   16 ounces water

Equipment

Newspapers   Shoe box or shallow pan
Rubber gloves   Wooden spoon
Cooking thermometer   Waxed paper or plastic wrap

Steps

1. Cover table with newspaper. Wear rubber gloves.
2. Put oil and vegetable shortening in a large glass or stainless steel pot (not aluminum).
3. Heat mixture on lowest setting. Stir with wooden spoon.
4. In a small glass or stainless steel pot, dissolve lye flakes in the 16 ounces of water.
5. Use a cooking thermometer to see that mixtures in both pans reach 96 degrees. Lye and water mixture will get hotter; let it cool down to 96 degrees.
6. Slowly pour lye mixture into oil mixture, stirring constantly.
7. Stir until thick, about 15 minutes.
8. Line a shoe box or shallow pan with waxed paper or plastic wrap.
9. Pour soap mixture into box or pan.
10. Let soap harden for 24 hours.
11. Cut the soap brick into smaller pieces.
12. Allow soap to sit for at least 2 weeks before using it.

From *Cooking Up U.S. History*, Second Edition. © 1999 Suzanne I. Barchers and Patricia C. Marden. Teacher Ideas Press. (800) 237-6124.

DIPPED CANDLES

Caution: Keep baking soda handy to smother flames should paraffin ignite.

Ingredients
1 pound paraffin
Cotton string

Equipment
Newspapers
2 tall tin cans (1-pound coffee cans work well)
Saucepan
Fork

Steps
1. Spread newspaper on table.
2. Fill 1 tin can about ⅔ full of water and place in a saucepan. Fill the other can with cold water.
3. Fill the saucepan about half full of water and put over medium heat on the stove.
4. As the water in the saucepan begins to boil, add chunks of paraffin to the tin can inside the saucepan until the can is almost full.
5. As the wax melts, it forms a layer on top of the water. The wax needs to be just the right temperature. If it is too hot it will slide off the string. If it is too cool it will be too thick for dipping. Keep the pan on the stove at a low heat.
6. Cut a piece of string twice as long as the can.
7. Lay the string over the prongs of a fork so that both sides hang down equally. Take the portion that lies over the fork and weave it among the prongs to hold the string in place.
8. Dip the string into the can until it touches the bottom.
9. Pull the string out of the can and dip it in the can of cold water to harden.
10. Continue dipping the string into the can of wax and then cold water until candles are as thick as desired.
11. Trim the cotton wicks to about ½ inch before burning candles.

Makes 6 medium candles.

MOLDED CANDLES

Caution: Keep baking soda handy to smother flames should paraffin ignite.

Ingredients
Paraffin
Cotton string

Equipment
Cardboard containers
Double boiler
Pencil

Steps
1. Melt paraffin in top of double boiler over low to medium heat.
2. Cut string about 4 inches longer than cardboard container.
3. Cut off the top of the container. Poke a hole in the bottom and thread the cut string through the hole. On the outside of the carton (bottom), knot the string to hold it in place.
4. Turn container right side up and tie the other end of string onto a pencil that has been laid across the top of the container. The string should be taut.
5. Pour melted wax into the cardboard container, almost to the top.
6. After the wax has cooled and hardened thoroughly, remove from container by dipping it in hot water for about 10 seconds and inverting the container.
7. Remove pencil and cut off excess string.

CANDLE CLOCK

Equipment
2 or more fat candles the same height and thickness
2 jar lids
Pencil or permanent marker

Steps
1. Use the jar lids as candle holders by dripping wax in the center of them and standing the candles up in the wax.
2. Place the 2 candles (on jar lids) side by side.
3. Have a clock nearby to measure the time.
4. Light one of the candles. After 1 hour, place a mark on the other candle at exactly the remaining height of the burning candle. Make another mark the same way after each hour until the first candle has burned all the way down.
5. Write a number by each mark on the candle to mark the hours.
6. Use the marked candle to mark other candles, making your own candle clocks.

Library Links

Library Link 1:   Where do oats come from? What other uses were there for oats? Why was it important to the early colonists to have a good supply of oats?

Library Link 2:   How did hasty pudding get its name?

Library Link 3:   What word did the Native American Indians use for corn? Did the early colonists use corn before they came to America? Why or why not?

Library Link 4:   Our cornmeal looks like flour and comes in a bag or carton. How did the early colonists prepare cornmeal? Why did they use corn-meal instead of wheat flour?

Library Link 5:   How did the colonists' diet change from what they ate in England? Why?

Library Link 6:   The recipe for corn sticks uses molasses for sweetener; however, such sweeteners were scarce in the 1600s. Find out how the Pilgrims sweetened their desserts and vegetables when they had no sugar, honey, or molasses.

Library Link 7:   Who brought ole kooks to the colonies?

Library Link 8:   Keep track of how much butter your family consumes in one week. Decide how many hours would be used to make a week's worth of butter for your family based on how long it took your class to make butter. Then decide how much time it would take to obtain the necessary ingredients for butter.

Library Link 9:   To what family does the bean plant belong? What other commonly eaten plants belong to this family? Why did the colonists rely on these plants?

Library Link 10:   When is squash harvested? Of what importance was the harvesting season to the early colonists?

Library Link 11:   A chowder is a kind of soup or stew. What is another popular kind of chowder? In what areas of the United States are chowders most popular? Why?

Library Link 12:   The Pilgrims learned how to make succotash from the Native American Indians who grew the beans and corn together in the same patch. How could this dish be made available in the winter? How would the preparation change?

Library Link 13:   How did the Pilgrims learn about pumpkins? Pumpkins have been featured in many stories and poems throughout our history. Find stories that have pumpkins in them.

Library Link 14:   The colonists not only made their own inks, but also made their own quills. Find out how this was done.

Library Link 15:   Colonists also made their own paper. Find out how this was done. Find examples of contemporary artists who have returned to the art of making paper. (Ask your art teacher for help.) Consider making paper for an extra project.

Library Link 16:   The colonists used all available resources to survive. Ashes were used to make lye, and nuts and berries were used for ink. Use the library to find other examples of how the colonists utilized and conserved materials.

Library Link 17:   We can buy paraffin for making candles. How did the colonists obtain the materials for making candles?

Library Link 18:   How did the colonists obtain molds for their molded candles? Did all colonists have molded candles? Why or why not?

Library Link 19:   Figure out how many candles your family would need each week to have three hours of candlelight every evening.

Bibliography—The Colonial Period

Nonfiction—Series

Colonial Histories. Nashville, Tenn.: Thomas Nelson, varying dates. Teacher resource or older students.

This series traces the histories of the 13 colonies from their earliest days through the Revolutionary War. Photographs, prints, maps, documents, and personal accounts enhance the narratives.

The Colony Series. New York: Franklin Watts, varying dates. Grades 3 and up.

This series features individual books about the 13 colonies: Connecticut, Delaware, Georgia, Maryland, Massachusetts, New Hampshire, New Jersey, New York, North Carolina, Pennsylvania, Rhode Island, South Carolina, and Virginia. The authors vary.

Fisher, Leonard Everett. *Colonial American Craftsman.* New York: Franklin Watts, varying dates. All grades.

Each of the following craftsmen is a title in the series, simply presented in fewer than 50 pages: Wigmakers, Weavers, Tanners, Silversmiths, Shoemakers, Shipbuilders, School Masters, Printers, Potters, Peddlers, Papermakers, Architects, Homemakers, Hatters, Glassmakers, Doctors, Cabinetmakers, and Blacksmiths.

Nonfiction—Individual Titles

Christmas in Colonial and Early America. Chicago: World Book, 1996. Grades 4 and up.

Drawn from the *World Book Encyclopedia,* this resource covers a variety of topics related to Christmas observations during colonial times.

Cobb, Mary. *The Quilt-Block History of Pioneer Days: With Projects Kids Can Make.* Illustrated by Jan Davey Ellis. Brookfield, Conn.: Millbrook Press, 1995. Grades 3 and up.

The contextual history of various types of quilts is described through text and color illustrations. The projects give this an added usefulness.

Fritz, Jean. *What's the Big Idea, Ben Franklin?* Illustrated by Margot Tomes. New York: Putnam, 1976. Grades 3 and up.

Ben Franklin's eccentricities and inventions are discussed in this lively biography. The amusing illustrations add interest to the reading.

———. *Who's That Stepping on Plymouth Rock?* Illustrated by J. B. Handelsman. New York: Coward-McCann, 1975. Grades 3 and up.

The history of the sometimes humorous, sometimes reverent treatment of Plymouth Rock is described with flare by Fritz.

Johnson, Sylvia A. *Tomatoes, Potatoes, Corn, and Beans: How the Foods of the Americas Changed Eating Around the World.* New York: Atheneum, 1997. Grades 6 and up.

An astonishing number of foods were first grown by Native American Indians and then transported to other parts of the world by the early European settlers. Photos, maps, and drawings enhance this overview of a fascinating topic.

Lizon, Karen Helene. *Colonial American Holidays and Entertainment.* New York: Franklin Watts, 1993. Grades 4 and up.

This resource describes holidays, games, amusements, sports, observances, and working bees. This is excellent for research and as a teacher resource.

Maestro, Betsy. *The New Americans: Colonial Times, 1620–1689.* Illustrated by Giulio Maestro. New York: Lothrop, Lee & Shepard, 1998. Grades 3 and up.

Maestro presents the period when the resources of America became of great interest to people from many countries, such as the Dutch, French, Spanish, and English.

Penner, Lucille Recht. *Eating the Plates: A Pilgrim Book of Food and Manners.* New York: Macmillan, 1991. Grades 4 and up.

The Pilgrims had to learn to like the food available to them when they arrived in the New World. Photographs and line drawings enhance this rich resource of their food and customs.

Perl, Lila. *Slumps, Grunts, and Snickerdoodles: What Colonial America Ate and Why.* Illustrated by Richard Cuffari. Boston: Houghton Mifflin, 1975. Grades 4 and up.

The importance of food in relation to colonial times is thoroughly discussed by Perl. The key recipes of the period are included.

Roop, Connie, and Peter Roop, editors. *Pilgrim Voices: Our First Year in the New World.* Illustrated by Shelley Pritchett. New York: Walker, 1995. Grades 3 and up.

Color illustrations highlight selected excerpts from the journals of the Pilgrims of the Plymouth Colony.

San Souci, Robert. *N. C. Wyeth's Pilgrims.* Illustrated by N. C. Wyeth. San Francisco: Chronicle Books, 1991. All ages.

The story of the Pilgrims' arrival, the settling of the Plymouth Colony, the first Thanksgiving, and daily life are described through text and illustrations.

Fiction

Avi. *Finding Providence.* Illustrated by James Watling. New York: HarperCollins, 1997. Grades 1 and up.

In 1635, Roger Williams is tried for preaching for equality and freedom of speech. He is sentenced to return to England, but escapes. The Narrangansett Indians invite him to bring his family to join them in what becomes the settlement of Providence, Rhode Island.

Fleming, Candace. *The Hatmaker's Sign: A Story by Benjamin Franklin.* Illustrated by Robert Andrew Parker. New York: Orchard, 1998. Grades 1 and up.

When Thomas Jefferson struggled with the changes demanded of him during the writing of the Declaration of Independence, Benjamin Franklin told him a story of a hatmaker who struggled to get the perfect sign written for his establishment.

Holmes, Mary Z. *Two Chimneys.* Austin, Tex.: Raintree Steck-Vaughn, 1992. Grades 4 and up.

Katherine arrives in Virginia with her family in 1622 at age seven. She enjoys the challenges of the tobacco plantation and, upon becoming a young lady, resists returning to England to marry.

Lasky, Kathryn. *A Journey to the New World: The Diary of Remember Patience Whipple.* New York: Scholastic, 1996. Grades 4 and up.

Students who enjoy reading a diary format will enjoy this story of Remember's experience on the *Mayflower* and at the Plimoth settlement.

Paul, Ann Whitford. *Eight Hands Round: A Patchwork Alphabet.* Illustrated by Jeanette Winter. New York: HarperCollins, 1991. Grades 1 and up.

The practice of making patchwork quilts is described in this lovely alphabet book. Each type of quilt is described and illustrated.

San Souci, Robert D. *The Red Heels.* Illustrated by Gary Kelley. New York: Dial, 1996. Grades 2 and up.

When a cobbler falls in love with a young woman whose shoes allow her to dance on the wind, he stays with her, joining in her nightly dancing. He finally misses his work and leaves her, only to have her follow, asking for a pair of sturdy shoes.

Stamper, Judith Bauer. *New Friends in a New Land: A Thanksgiving Story.* Illustrated by Chet Jezierski. Austin, Tex.: Raintree Steck-Vaughn, 1993. Grades kindergarten and up.

Damaris Hopkins lives with her family in Plymouth village in 1621. The friendship with Squanto and the Wampanoags is described, leading up to the first Thanksgiving.

Waters, Kate. *On the Mayflower: Voyage of the Ship's Apprentice and a Passenger Girl.* Photographs by Russ Kendall. New York: Scholastic, 1996. All ages.

When William Small, the ship's apprentice, sails to America, he meets Ellen Moore, a young girl who is traveling alone. Photographed on the *Mayflower II,* this is a fascinating portrayal of that first voyage.

———. *Samuel Eaton's Day: A Day in the Life of a Pilgrim Boy.* Photographs by Russ Kendall. New York: Scholastic, 1993. All ages.

Based on life during 1627 and photographed at Plimoth Plantation, a living history museum in Plymouth, Massachusetts, this is the story of a young boy's first time helping with the rye harvest.

———. *Sarah Morton's Day: A Day in the Life of a Pilgrim Girl.* Photographs by Russ Kendall. New York: Scholastic, 1989. All ages.

Similar in format to *Samuel Eaton's Day,* this story follows Sarah through a typical day for a young Pilgrim girl in 1627.

From *Cooking Up U.S. History*, Second Edition. © 1999 Suzanne I. Barchers and Patricia C. Marden. Teacher Ideas Press. (800) 237-6124.

CD-ROMs

The American Girls Premiere. Minneapolis, Minn.: The Learning Company, 1997. Grades 4 and up.

    This multimedia theater production tool with characters from the American Girls books includes a focus on Colonial America.

Colonial America. Washington, D.C.: National Geographic, 1997. Grades 4 and up.

    Travel with the settlers as they come to the New World. Learn what their lives were like in the colonies.

Kits

The Tinsmith Workshop. Española, N.Mex.: Juniper Learning. (800-456-1776.)

    Includes materials and tools for tinsmithing, learning materials, instruction booklet, and ESL strategies.

Who Were the Pilgrims? Washington, D.C.: National Geographic, 1989. Grades K-2.

    Kit includes a cassette, student booklets, reproducibles, library catalog cards, and teacher's guide.

Videos

Star-Spangled Banner: Our Nation's Flag. Washington, D.C.: National Geographic, 1996. 20 minutes. Grades 4 and up.

    Learn about our nation's flag from the original to the present-day design.

What's the Big Idea, Ben Franklin? Norwalk, Conn.: Weston Woods, n.d. 30 minutes. Grades 2 and up.

    Jean Fritz's book about Ben Franklin's love of life is captured on this video. Illustrated by Margot Tomes.

Where Do You Think You're Going, Christopher Columbus? Norwalk, Conn.: Weston Woods, n.d. 32 minutes. Grades 3 and up.

    With humor and insight, Jean Fritz narrates her book about Christopher Columbus's journey to America.

3
The Revolutionary War

The Revolutionary War

Word List

- Apples
- Boston Tea Party
- Congressional Bean Soup
- Declaration of Independence
- Election Cake
- Federal Cake
- Guinea fowl
- Hogshead
- Independence Cake
- Jefferson
- King George III
- *Liberty*
- Minutemen
- Nuts
- Onions
- Pickled beef
- Quartering Act
- Rum
- Stamp Act
- Tobacco
- Unfree labor
- Valley Forge
- Washington
- X
- Yorktown
- Zane, Elizabeth

Tapping Trees for Maple Syrup

The Native American Indians originally taught the settlers how to tap maple trees for the sap in order to make maple syrup and maple sugar. Trees must be tapped in early spring, just as the snow begins to thaw. Sugar maple or black maple trees provide the largest quantities of sap. A spout is hammered into the tree, creating about a ½-inch hole, and a bucket is hung from it. After the sap is collected in the bucket, it is boiled until most of the water has evaporated and a thick syrup is left.

MAPLE SYRUP CANDY

Ingredients and Equipment
Maple syrup
Snow

Steps
1. Cook maple syrup over medium heat in a saucepan until it reaches 275 degrees or the hard ball stage (forms a hard ball when dropped in a cup of cold water).
2. Fill large cake pan with a mound of clean snow.
3. Slowly pour cooked syrup over snow, dribbling it in thin strips.
4. Let syrup cool.

SWEET POTATO CAKE

Ingredients

1 cup butter or margarine, softened
2 cups sugar
4 eggs
2 ¾ cups cooked,
    mashed sweet potatoes
3 cups flour
2 teaspoons baking powder

¾ teaspoon baking soda
1 teaspoon cinnamon
½ teaspoon nutmeg
½ teaspoon allspice
¼ teaspoon salt
2 teaspoons vanilla
1 cup chopped nuts (optional)

Steps
1. Cream butter and stir in sugar.
2. Add eggs, beating well after each one.
3. Add sweet potato and mix thoroughly.
4. Mix together in a separate bowl the flour, baking powder, soda, cinnamon, nutmeg, allspice, and salt.
5. Slowly add dry flour mixture to sweet potato mixture, stirring well.
6. Stir in vanilla.
7. Add nuts, if desired.
8. Pour batter into a greased, 10-inch tube pan.
9. Bake for 1 hour and 10 minutes at 350 degrees or until done.

Serves 10 to 12.

From *Cooking Up U.S. History*, Second Edition. © 1999 Suzanne I. Barchers and Patricia C. Marden. Teacher Ideas Press. (800) 237-6124.

SWEET POTATO PUDDING

Ingredients

2 cups raw, grated sweet potato
1 ½ cups water
⅓ cup sugar
¼ teaspoon cinnamon
¼ teaspoon allspice
4 tablespoons melted margarine

Steps

1. Combine the potato with the water, sugar, cinnamon, and allspice.
2. Stir in the melted margarine.
3. Grease a 1-quart casserole dish.
4. Pour the mixture into the dish.
5. Cover the dish with aluminum foil and bake at 350 degrees for 30 minutes.
6. Uncover the dish and bake for about 30 minutes more or until a knife inserted in the center comes out clean.

Serves 6.

CORNMEAL SPOON BREAD

Ingredients

1 ¾ cups milk
¼ teaspoon salt
⅔ cup cornmeal
3 tablespoons butter
2 eggs

Steps

1. Boil milk in a medium-sized saucepan.
2. Add salt.
3. Stir in cornmeal and continue to stir until mixture thickens.
4. Add butter and stir.
5. Remove mixture from heat.
6. Beat eggs well and then stir into cornmeal mixture.
7. Butter a 9-inch square baking pan.
8. Pour mixture into the pan.
9. Bake at 375 degrees for 1 hour.

Makes 9 1-inch square pieces.

From *Cooking Up U.S. History*, Second Edition. © 1999 Suzanne I. Barchers and Patricia C. Marden. Teacher Ideas Press. (800) 237-6124.

CORN PUDDING

Ingredients

¼ cup cornmeal
1 ½ cups cold milk
2 ½ cups heated milk
½ stick margarine

¾ cup molasses
½ teaspoon cinnamon
¼ teaspoon salt
2 well-beaten eggs

Steps

1. In the bottom half of a double boiler, heat water until it boils.
2. In the top of a double boiler, stir cornmeal into 1 cup of the cold milk.
3. Stir in the 2 ½ cups of heated milk.
4. Cook and stir until smooth.
5. Cover the pan.
6. Lower heat so that the water simmers lightly. Cook for 25 to 30 minutes.
7. Remove from heat.
8. Stir in the rest of the ingredients.
9. Pour the mixture into a buttered 2-quart baking pan.
10. Pour the remaining cold milk on top.
11. Bake at 350 degrees for about 1 hour or until firm.

Serves 4 to 6.

CHESS PIE

Ingredients

½ cup margarine or butter
1 cup brown sugar
3 eggs
⅓ cup evaporated milk
¾ cup chopped nuts (pecans or walnuts)
¾ cup raisins
½ cup chopped dates
½ teaspoon vanilla
⅓ cup orange juice
1 9-inch pastry shell, unbaked

Steps

1. Cream the butter.
2. Stir in sugar and eggs until smooth and creamy.
3. Stir in milk, nuts, raisins, dates, vanilla, and orange juice.
4. Pour mixture in the pie shell.
5. Bake pie for 10 minutes at 450 degrees.
6. Reduce heat to 325 degrees and bake about 25 minutes.

Serves 8.

From *Cooking Up U.S. History*, Second Edition. © 1999 Suzanne I. Barchers and Patricia C. Marden. Teacher Ideas Press. (800) 237-6124.

MINCEMEAT PIE

Ingredients

2 pounds cooked beef, finely chopped
4 cups apples, peeled and finely chopped
1 pound raisins
1 box currants
½ pound brown sugar
2 cups molasses
4 ½ cups cider

1 ½ teaspoons salt
1 ½ teaspoons pepper
1 ½ teaspoons allspice
1 ½ teaspoons ground cloves
2 tablespoons cinnamon
1 tablespoon nutmeg
2 unbaked pie crusts

Steps

1. Put meat in a very large saucepan and cover with water.
2. Simmer meat over low heat until tender and almost dry.
3. Mix all other ingredients together in a large bowl.
4. Add ingredients to the meat. If the pan is too small, divide the ingredients in half and use 2 pans.
5. Bring to a boil over medium heat and simmer for 20 minutes.
6. Divide ingredients in half and put half in each pie crust.
7. Bake at 375 degrees for 40 to 50 minutes or until crust is browned.

Makes 2 large pies.

VIRGINIA POUNDCAKE

Ingredients

2 cups butter
2 cups sugar
9 eggs
1 ½ teaspoons vanilla

½ teaspoon nutmeg
2 tablespoons orange juice
4 cups flour

Steps

1. Cream butter.
2. Using an electric mixer, beat in sugar until smooth and creamy (or beat by hand for 5 minutes).
3. Beat eggs in a separate bowl until thick and light yellow.
4. Add eggs to butter mixture and mix very well (or beat by hand for 5 minutes).
5. Beat in vanilla, nutmeg, and orange juice.
6. While mixer is running, beat in flour, a small amount at a time (or beat very well by hand).
7. Grease 2 9-inch loaf pans.
8. Pour half of the mixture into each pan.
9. Bake at 325 degrees for about 1 hour or until a toothpick inserted in the center comes out clean.

Serves 15 to 20.

From *Cooking Up U.S. History*, Second Edition. © 1999 Suzanne I. Barchers and Patricia C. Marden. Teacher Ideas Press. (800) 237-6124.

COTTAGE CHEESE

Ingredients
½ gallon skim milk
⅓ cup fresh cultured buttermilk
Water

Equipment
1 dairy thermometer
1 long stainless steel knife
1 large pan or kettle
A rack to fit in the bottom of the large pan
A stainless steel or enamel bowl or pan that fits into the large pan
Muslin sack or cheesecloth

Steps
1. Let skim milk and buttermilk sit out until they reach room temperature (70 to 75 degrees).
2. Stir buttermilk into skim milk in stainless steel pan.
3. Let stand 12 to 14 hours until clabbered (soured and separated).
4. Cut through clabbered milk with a stainless steel knife at ½-inch intervals, first down, then across, then diagonally. Cut all the way to the bottom. This is the curd.
5. Let stand for 10 minutes.
6. Add 1 quart of 100-degree water to curd.
7. Set the pan with the curd in it on the rack in the larger pan that has been one-third filled with water.
8. Heat until the curd reaches 100 degrees. Keep it at this temperature for about 45 minutes, stirring every 5 minutes.
9. As you stir, the whey (liquid) will be forced out and the curds will settle to the bottom.
10. Curds are cooked when they break between the fingers without leaving a milky liquid on the fingers.
11. Pour the curds and whey carefully into the muslin sack and rinse with cold water.
12. Let drain until liquid stops dripping.
13. A small amount of cream may be stirred into curds if they are too dry.
14. Cover and store in the refrigerator.

Serves 6.

From *Cooking Up U.S. History*, Second Edition. © 1999 Suzanne I. Barchers and Patricia C. Marden. Teacher Ideas Press. (800) 237-6124.

FRUIT JELLY

Ingredients
3 pounds of fruit, to yield about 4 cups of juice
    (no pineapple or quince)
¾ cup sugar for each cup of juice

Equipment
Large saucepan
Colander
Cheesecloth
Jars
Paraffin
Small saucepan
Large bowl
Teakettle full of water
Hot pad mittens (to lift jars of hot water)

Steps
1. Wash the fruit and cut it into small pieces. (Do not peel or core.)
2. Put fruit in saucepan and cook until it creates juice, in about 5 to 15 minutes. If necessary, add some water to keep fruit from burning.
3. Strain fruit through a colander into a bowl.
4. Wash colander and place it over the second large bowl.
5. Pour the juice from the first bowl through several layers of cheesecloth draped over the colander.
6. Let the juice drip through for about an hour.
7. Measure juice by the cup into the saucepan.
8. Boil juice for 5 minutes.
9. Add ¾ cup of sugar for each cup of fruit juice.
10. Boil mixture for 15 to 30 minutes or until mixture jells or thickens. Test to see if it has jelled by putting a few drops in the freezer for a few minutes to see if it gets thick when cooled.
11. Boil water in the teakettle.
12. Pour boiling water into jars, and then immediately empty the jars and fill them with jelly.
13. Melt paraffin in a saucepan over very low heat.
14. Pour about ½ inch of melted paraffin over the top of each jar of jelly. Let it cool.
15. Jars are now sealed and can be stored in a cool, dry place.

APPLE BUTTER

Ingredients
Apples (enough to equal 4 cups of sieved fruit)
¾ cup sugar or honey
¾ teaspoon cinnamon
2 tablespoons margarine or butter (melted)

Steps
1. Wash and quarter apples.
2. Remove cores and stems.
3. Put apples in a large kettle.
4. Add about 1 inch water.
5. Cover kettle and cook until fruit is soft.
6. Put apples through a food mill or colander.
7. Measure 4 cups of fruit into a 9-by-13-inch baking pan.
8. Add sugar or honey, cinnamon, and margarine. Stir well.
9. Bake at 300 degrees.
10. Stir every 30 minutes.
11. Bake until thick.

MINT TEA

Ingredients
⅔ cup mint leaves
4 cups water
Sugar
Lemon

Steps
1. Wash, drain, and chop mint leaves.
2. Put leaves into a teapot.
3. Boil water and pour over the leaves.
4. Let tea steep for 10 minutes.
5. Serve with sugar and lemon.

Serves 4.

From *Cooking Up U.S. History*, Second Edition. © 1999 Suzanne I. Barchers and Patricia C. Marden. Teacher Ideas Press. (800) 237-6124.

Library Links

Library Link 1:   What does "Sap's rising!" mean? Read *Sugaring Time* by Kathryn Lasky (New York: Macmillan, 1983) and write a report about making maple syrup today.

Library Link 2:   The recipe for sweet potato cake has several spices in it: vanilla, cinnamon, nutmeg, and allspice. Why are spices important in history? Why were spices heavily used in meat?

Library Link 3:   How are sweet potatoes different from white potatoes? Why did the colonists eat so many sweet potatoes?

Library Link 4:   Today we set our ovens to the temperature we need to bake our foods. The colonists did not have electric or gas ovens. How did they bake? What problems did they have? How might they try to solve them?

Library Link 5:   Puddings are used in folk and fairy tales and nursery rhymes. Find as many stories with puddings in them as you can. Extra challenge: what is a pudding stone?

Library Link 6:   What is a pudding cap?

Library Link 7:   Find out why chess pie has its name. (Hint: chess is believed to have come from the word *chest*.)

Library Link 8:   Mincemeat pies were made well ahead of the holidays and set aside. In America, meat was plentiful for mincemeat pies. What did they use more of in England?

Library Link 9:   Find out why Virginia pound cake is called a pound cake. In early 1774, why did ladies have tea parties without tea?

Library Link 10:   What famous nursery rhyme talks about curds and whey, the parts of cottage cheese found in the recipe? When were the first cows brought to America?

Library Link 11:   What kinds of berries did the colonists find available to them?

Library Link 12:   Johnny Appleseed was born in 1774. What was his real name? When did he begin planting apple trees?

Library Link 13:   After a fine dinner or a ball in a colonial city, how might the guests spend the remainder of the evening?

From *Cooking Up U.S. History*, Second Edition. © 1999 Suzanne I. Barchers and Patricia C. Marden. Teacher Ideas Press. (800) 237-6124.

Bibliography—The Revolutionary War

Nonfiction

Adler, David A. *A Picture Book of George Washington.* Illustrated by John and Alexandra Wallner. New York: Holiday House, 1989. All ages.
This simple, colorful picture book gives an overview of the life of George Washington. This is a good read-aloud for the very young.

Clinton, Susan. *The Story of the Green Mountain Boys.* Chicago: Childrens Press, 1987. Grades 3 and up.
Led by Ethan Allen, the Green Mountain Boys fought against the British in various northern areas of the colonies. The text is straightforward with photographs and art of the period.

Fritz, Jean. *And Then What Happened, Paul Revere?* Illustrated by Margot Tomes. New York: Coward, McCann & Geoghegan, 1973. Grades 2 and up.
Jean Fritz intersperses the story of Paul Revere with humorous tidbits and anecdotes. For example, Paul's children were named Deborah, Paul, Sarah, Mary, Frances, Elizabeth (from his first wife) and Joshua, Joseph, Harriet, Maria, and John (from his second wife).

———. *Can't You Make Them Behave, King George?* Illustrated by Tomie dePaola. New York: Coward, McCann & Geoghegan, 1977. Grades 3 and up.
Americans often assume King George III was primarily a tyrant. Fritz's biography provides a more balanced, entertaining, view of King George.

———. *Shh! We're Writing the Constitution.* Illustrated by Tomie dePaola. New York: Putnam, 1987. Grades 3 and up.
Writing the Constitution was a necessary challenge, and Fritz describes the process with humorous and engrossing details.

———. *Where Was Patrick Henry on the 29th of May?* Illustrated by Margot Tomes. New York: Coward, McCann & Geoghegan, 1975. Grades 3 and up.
Another humorous look at one of the well-known Revolutionary War figures is provided by Fritz. Henry's flair for drama and his ability to capitalize on any situation he encountered are described with intriguing details.

———. *Why Don't You Get a Horse, Sam Adams?* Illustrated by Trina Schart Hyman. New York: Coward, McCann & Geoghegan, 1974. Grades 3 and up.
Sam Adams was willing to dress up a bit when talking to people about the English government and the need to fight for independence, but he drew the line at riding a horse.

———. *Will You Sign Here, John Hancock?* Illustrated by Trina Schart Hyman. New York: Coward, McCann & Geoghegan, 1975. Grades 3 and up.
John Hancock's refusal to pay taxes to King George and his general flamboyancy, including his signing of the Declaration of Independence, are described.

Giblin, James Cross. *Fireworks, Picnics, and Flags: The Story of the Fourth of July Symbols.* Illustrated by Ursula Arndt. New York: Clarion Books, 1983. Grades 3 and up.
    The history of the events surrounding the Revolutionary War is presented through a discussion of the symbols of the Fourth of July. Included are chapters on the Centennial Exhibition of 1876 and the Bicentennial of 1976.

Goor, Ron, and Nancy Goor. *Williamsburg: Cradle of the Revolution.* New York: Macmillan, 1994. Grades 3 and up.
    A liberal assortment of photographs of Williamsburg enhance the text that describes life in Colonial Williamsburg as the Revolution begins.

Lasky, Kathryn. *Sugaring Time.* New York: Macmillan, 1983.
    Black-and-white photographs highlight this factual narrative of the process of gathering maple syrup.

Maestro, Betsy, and Giulio Maestro. *A More Perfect Union: The Story of Our Constitution.* New York: Lothrop, Lee & Shepard Books, 1987. Grades 1 and up.
    The events surrounding the writing and ratification of the Constitution are described with text and large watercolors.

Martin, Joseph Plumb. *Yankee Doodle Boy.* Edited by George F. Scheer. New York: Holiday House, 1995. Grades 6 and up.
    Joseph Martin enlisted at the age of 15 in 1776. After seven years of service he recorded his experiences at battles, the harsh conditions, and the occasional humorous events.

Meltzer, Milton, editor. *The American Revolutionaries: A History in Their Own Words, 1750–1800.* New York: Thomas Y. Crowell, 1987. Grades 4 and up.
    "In letters, diaries, journals, memoirs, interviews, ballads, newspapers, pamphlets and speeches we find the first person evidence of life" from 1750–1800. Americans of all ages and backgrounds communicate about their own experiences. This is an excellent resource to use when relating war to human beings.

Fiction

Anderson, Joan. *1787.* Illustrated by Alexander Farquharson. San Diego, Calif.: Harcourt Brace Jovanovich, 1987. Grades 5 and up.
    As aide to James Madison, Jared becomes involved in the framing of the Constitution and the making of history.

Avi. *Captain Grey.* New York: Pantheon, 1977. Grades 4 and up.
    A young boy is captured by pirates during the Revolutionary War.

———. *The Fighting Ground.* New York: Harper and Row, 1984. Grades 5 and up.
    Jonathan is only 13, but he runs away to join the Revolutionary War effort as a soldier. Thoughts of being a hero are forgotten as he faces capture and death.

Bourne, Miriam Anne. *Uncle George Washington and Harriot's Guitar.* Illustrated by Elise
  Primavera. New York: Coward-McCann, 1983. Grades 3 and up.
  Eleven-year-old Harriot was an orphan, relying upon the generosity of her relatives. In cor-
respondence with her famous uncle, she requests a guitar. His response and actions provide another view of Washington.

Collier, James Lincoln, and Christopher Collier. *Jump Ship to Freedom.* New York: Dell, 1996.
  Grades 4 and up.
  Daniel Arabus and his mother are slaves, even though their father, by fighting in the war,
earned enough money in notes to buy their freedom. When his father dies, the notes are taken and
Daniel steals them back. He is forced to board a ship and must struggle to return to his family and
gain their freedom. (Post-Revolutionary War.)

————. *my brother Sam is dead.* New York: Scholastic Book Services, 1974. Grades 4 and up.
  The futility of war is poignantly demonstrated when this family is torn between the opposing
forces and Sam is killed tragically by his compatriots.

————. *War Comes to Willy Freeman.* New York: Delacorte Press, 1983. Grades 4 and up.
  After Willy's father is killed by Redcoats and her mother is taken prisoner, she disguises
herself as a boy and sets out in search of her mother.

————. *Who Is Carrie?* New York: Delacorte Press, 1984. Grades 4 and up.
  Carrie, a slave in Sam Fraunce's Tavern in New York City, is unaware of her heritage. When
Daniel Arabus (see *Jump Ship to Freedom*) comes to the tavern, Carrie agrees to help him, learn-
ing about her family in the process. (Post-Revolutionary War.)

————. *The Winter Hero.* New York: Four Winds Press, 1978. Grades 4 and up.
  It is 1787 and Justin is part of Shay's Rebellion, a farmers' revolt against the Massachusetts
taxes. (Post-Revolutionary War.)

Fleming, Candace. *The Hatmaker's Sign: A Story by Benjamin Franklin.* Illustrated by Robert
  Andrew Parker. New York: Orchard, 1998. Grades 1 and up.
  When Thomas Jefferson struggled with the changes demanded of him during the writing of
the Declaration of Independence, Benjamin Franklin told him a story of a hatmaker who struggled to get the perfect sign written for his establishment.

Forbes, Esther. *Johnny Tremain.* Illustrated by Lynd Ward. New York: Dell, 1968. Grades 5 and
  up.
  This challenging Newbery book is about a young man's experiences during the Revolutionary War. In contrast to the rural setting of *my brother Sam is dead* (see Collier annotation in this
list), this book is set in the city.

O'Dell, Scott. *Sarah Bishop.* Boston: Houghton Mifflin, 1980. Grades 5 and up.
  Sarah loses her brother to the war and her father is a prisoner. She is taken prisoner by the
British but manages to escape.

Rappaport, Doreen. *The Boston Coffee Party.* Illustrated by Emily Arnold McCully. New York: Harper and Row, 1988. Grades 1 and up.
> This easy-to-read book tells the story of the Boston women's revolt against Merchant Thomas, who is overcharging them for sugar and coffee.

Robinet, Harriette Gillem. *Washington City Is Burning.* New York: Simon & Schuster, 1996. Grades 4 and up.
> Virginia has come to work at the White House in 1814, just when the British burn much of the city. Her work also includes helping slaves escape to freedom, and her bravery is demonstrated in this rich story.

CD-ROM

The American Revolution. Washington, D.C.: National Geographic, 1996. Grades 4 and up.
> Explores the American resistance to the British.

Kit

Who Was George Washington? Washington, D.C.: National Geographic, 1993. Grades kindergarten through 2.
> Kit includes a cassette, student booklets, reproducibles, library catalog cards, and teacher's guide.

Videos

And Then What Happened, Paul Revere? Norwalk, Conn.: Weston Woods, n.d. 30 minutes. Grades 2 and up.
> Jean Fritz's book is captured in this video of Paul Revere's story.

Jean Fritz: Six Revolutionary War Figures. Norwalk, Conn.: Weston Woods, n.d. 16 minutes. Grades 4 and up.
> Using characters from Fritz's biographies of Ben Franklin, Patrick Henry, Sam Adams, Paul Revere, John Hancock, and King George, the formation of the nation is described.

Johnny Tremain. Disney Educational Products, 1997. 81 minutes. Grades 4 and up.
> This is a video of Esther Forbes' novel.

Shh! We're Writing the Constitution. Norwalk, Conn.: Weston Woods, n.d. 31 minutes. Grades 4 and up.
> Jean Fritz introduces viewers to the 1887 summer convention and the efforts to draft the Constitution.

4
Westward Expansion

Westward Expansion

Word List

- Adventure
- Barn raisings; Boone, Daniel
- Chuckwagons, Conestoga wagons
- Deer leather
- Erie Canal
- Furs
- Gold
- Homesteading
- Immigrants
- Jerky
- Kissing bees
- Lewis and Clark
- Missouri Compromise
- Northwest Territory
- Oregon Trail
- Pawpaws
- Quest
- Rocky Mountains
- Sod houses
- Tree planting
- Union Pacific Railroad
- Vegetables
- Wilderness Road
- X
- Youngberry
- Zuni Native Americans

From *Cooking Up U.S. History*, Second Edition. © 1999 Suzanne I. Barchers and Patricia C. Marden. Teacher Ideas Press. (800) 237-6124.

SUN-DRIED FRUIT

Ingredients
Fruits (raspberries, plums, peaches, cherries, etc.)

Equipment
Cheesecloth
Cookie sheets

Steps
1. Wash fruit thoroughly.
2. If fruit has pits, cut fruit in half and remove pits. Slice larger fruit into pieces.
3. Spread the fruit on large cookie sheets.
4. Cover fruit with 1 layer of cheesecloth.
5. Place fruit outside in the sun. Leave it there all day, but take it inside at night.
6. Continue to put it outside each day until it dries up and becomes leathery, but not crisp.
7. Store in a tightly covered jar.

SOURDOUGH STARTER

Ingredients
½ teaspoon active dry yeast
½ cup very warm water
¾ cup flour
2 cups warm water (110 to 115 degrees)
2 ½ cups flour

Steps
1. Put first 3 ingredients in a large glass jar.
2. Stir well with a wooden spoon.
3. Let mixture sit uncovered for 5 to 6 days or until it bubbles and smells sour. Stir mixture each day.
4. When the mixture is ready, store in the refrigerator.

When you are ready to make biscuits, pancakes, or bread:

1. At least 10 hours before, add rest of the ingredients to the starter.
2. Mix until lumpy.
3. Let the mixture sit out overnight, covered.
4. Remove 1 cup for the next starter and store in refrigerator.
5. Use remainder of starter for your recipe. (Recipes for sourdough biscuits and pancakes follow.)

SOURDOUGH BISCUITS

Ingredients

¾ cup sourdough starter (see page 53)
1 cup milk
3 cups flour

½ teaspoon salt
1 tablespoon sugar
½ teaspoon baking soda

Steps

1. Use warm bubbly starter. Put it in a large bowl.
2. Add milk to starter.
3. Mix the flour, salt, sugar, and baking soda in another bowl.
4. Stir the flour mixture into the starter mixture.
5. Put dough onto a floured cloth or piece of waxed paper.
6. Roll dough out with a floured rolling pin until it is about ½-inch thick.
7. Cut biscuits out with a 2-inch floured cutter.
8. Place biscuits on a well-greased cookie sheet.
9. Cover biscuits with a slightly damp linen towel and place in a warm place to rise.
10. Let biscuits rise for about 30 minutes.
11. Bake biscuits in a 375 degree oven until slightly brown, about 10 to 15 minutes.

Makes 15.

SOURDOUGH PANCAKES

Ingredients

1 can evaporated milk
¾ cup water
2 cups flour
1 cup sourdough starter (see page 53)
6 eggs

2 tablespoons sugar
1 teaspoon salt
2 teaspoons baking soda
Butter, syrup, or confectioner's sugar

Steps

1. The night before making pancakes, mix evaporated milk, water, and 2 cups flour into 1 cup sourdough starter.
2. Mix well and cover. Leave out overnight.
3. The next morning heat griddle.
4. Add eggs, sugar, salt, and baking soda to sourdough mixture.
5. Mix well.
6. Grease the griddle lightly.
7. Pour spoonfuls of batter on the griddle.
8. Turn pancakes over when bubbles appear and pancakes are light brown.
9. Serve with butter and syrup or confectioner's sugar.

Makes 35 to 36 4-inch pancakes. To make a smaller batch of pancakes, follow steps 1 and 2. At step 3, separate the mixture into two equal parts. Refrigerate one portion for use another day. Proceed with steps 4 through 9, using 3 eggs, 1 tablespoon sugar, ½ teaspoon salt, and 1 teaspoon baking soda for the pancake batter.

From *Cooking Up U.S. History*, Second Edition. © 1999 Suzanne I. Barchers and Patricia C. Marden. Teacher Ideas Press. (800) 237-6124.

BAKING SODA BISCUITS

Ingredients
2 cups flour
1 ¼ teaspoons salt
1 teaspoon baking soda
2 tablespoons melted shortening
¾ cup sour milk*
Milk to brush tops of biscuits

Steps
1. Mix flour, salt, and soda in a large bowl.
2. Stir in shortening and milk until a soft dough forms. Add more milk if necessary.
3. Roll dough out on floured board to 1-inch thickness.
4. Cut out rounds of dough with 2-inch floured cutter.
5. Place biscuits so that sides touch on a greased cookie sheet.
6. Brush tops with plain milk.
7. Bake at 400 degrees for about 15 minutes or until lightly browned.

*To make sour milk, add 1 tablespoon of vinegar or lemon juice to milk and let sit for 10 minutes to curdle.

Makes 10 to 12.

CORN FRITTERS

Ingredients
1 #2 can corn (20 ounces)
2 eggs
½ cup milk
1 cup flour
1 teaspoon baking powder
1 teaspoon salt
1 teaspoon sugar
Vegetable oil for frying
Optional: syrup, butter, or confectioner's sugar

Steps
1. Strain corn and put it in a large mixing bowl.
2. Add eggs, milk, flour, baking powder, salt, and sugar. Stir until blended.
3. Heat oil in large frying pan or deep fat fryer over medium heat.
4. When oil is hot, drop 1 tablespoon of batter into the frying pan.
5. Cook 3 minutes and then turn and cook 3 minutes on the other side or until light brown.
6. Drain fritters on paper towels.
7. Serve with butter, maple syrup, or rolled in confectioner's sugar.

Makes 25 to 30.

COWBOY FRYING PAN BREAD

Ingredients
2 cups flour
2 teaspoons baking powder
1 ½ teaspoons salt
1 ¼ cups sugar

⅓ cup oil
Water
Butter or honey

Steps
1. Mix flour, baking powder, salt, and sugar in a large bowl.
2. Gradually stir in the oil and just enough water to make a light dough.
3. Knead the dough just enough to mix the ingredients.
4. Grease a 7- or 8-inch frying pan.
5. Cut off enough dough to spread it ½-inch thick in the bottom of the frying pan.
6. Poke a hole about 1 inch wide in the middle of the dough to let steam escape.
7. Place pan over a fire and cook until bottom of bread is browned.
8. Set pan in a vertical position in front of the fire. Be careful that bread doesn't slip out. Bread needs to face the fire. Turn pan so top browns evenly.
9. When bread is evenly browned, remove it from pan and serve warm with butter or honey.

Serves 4 to 6.

BAKED BEANS

Ingredients
1 ½ cups dried beans
Water
½ cup chopped onion
4 tablespoons molasses
3 tablespoons catsup

½ cup brown sugar
1 tablespoon mustard
1 teaspoon salt
¼ pound bacon

Steps
1. Put beans in a large pot and cover with water.
2. Soak beans for 1 hour.
3. Add 3 more cups of water.
4. Boil over low heat for 1 hour.
5. Preheat oven to 250 degrees.
6. Strain beans, but save the water.
7. Put beans in a casserole dish.
8. Add onion, molasses, catsup, brown sugar, mustard, salt, and bacon. Stir well.
9. Cover casserole dish and bake 6 to 9 hours or until beans are soft. (Check beans often and add some of the drained water if they become dry.)

Serves 4 to 6.

From *Cooking Up U.S. History*, Second Edition. © 1999 Suzanne I. Barchers and Patricia C. Marden. Teacher Ideas Press. (800) 237-6124.

COWBOY PIE

Ingredients
¼ cup shortening
1 beaten egg
½ cup milk
2 tablespoons oil
½ cup flour
¾ cup cornmeal
1 teaspoon baking powder
1 tablespoon sugar
¾ teaspoon salt
2 cans chili

Steps
1. Preheat oven to 400 degrees.
2. Melt shortening in a large saucepan.
3. Remove from heat and stir in egg, milk, and oil.
4. Stir in flour, cornmeal, baking powder, sugar, and salt.
5. Pour chili into an 8-inch square pan.
6. Pour batter over chili.
7. Bake in oven for 15 to 20 minutes.

Serves 4 to 6.

TACOS

Ingredients
12 taco shells
1 large can chili without beans
1 onion, finely chopped
2 cups shredded cheese
2 tomatoes, chopped
4 cups shredded lettuce
Picante sauce

Steps
1. Heat oven to 400 degrees.
2. Put taco shells on a cookie sheet.
3. Heat them for 4 minutes.
4. Meanwhile, heat chili in a saucepan until hot.
5. Put chopped onion, cheese, tomatoes, and lettuce in separate bowls.
6. Remove taco shells from oven and fill with chili, onion, cheese, tomatoes, and lettuce.
7. Pour picante sauce over fillings.

Serves 12.

WILTED LETTUCE SALAD

Ingredients
1 large head of lettuce
4 slices bacon
¼ cup vinegar
¼ cup sugar
½ teaspoon dry mustard
⅓ cup finely chopped onion

Steps
1. Wash and dry lettuce.
2. Tear lettuce into bite-sized pieces and put into large bowl.
3. Cut bacon into small pieces.
4. Fry bacon in heavy skillet over medium-high heat until crisp. Reduce heat to low.
5. Add vinegar, sugar, and mustard to skillet. Stir well until ingredients are heated through.
6. Mix onions with lettuce.
7. Stir bacon mixture into lettuce. Mix well.

Serves 4.

CRANBERRY JELLY

Ingredients
1 pound cranberries
1 ¼ cups water
2 ¼ cups sugar

Steps
1. Wash the cranberries.
2. Put the water in a large saucepan.
3. Add the sugar to the water and boil.
4. Add the berries.
5. Cook 15 to 20 minutes over low heat until berries are soft and mushy.
6. Serve hot or cold.

Serves 6.

Library Links

Library Link 1:   The Cherokee would grow fruits and vegetables during the summer and dry them in the sun or over fires for the winter. Find out how to make leather britches beans.

Library Link 2:   Why was a Canadian or Alaskan prospector called a *sourdough*? What were the staples of the prospector's diet?

Library Link 3:   Find the origins of sourdough.

Library Link 4:   Why was sourdough not used for many years?

Library Link 5:   What was baking soda called in the 1800s?

Library Link 6:   Travelers might use dried corn for recipes such as corn soup. How is corn dried?

Library Link 7:   What is the Mexican name for beans? How did pinto beans get their name?

Library Link 8:   Find out what a chuck wagon looked like. Draw a picture of one.

Library Link 9:   Research the origin and history of tomatoes.

Library Link 10:   New England Native American Indians called cranberries *sassamanesh*. Where in the United States do cranberries grow? What kind of environment is needed for cranberries?

From *Cooking Up U.S. History*, Second Edition. © 1999 Suzanne I. Barchers and Patricia C. Marden. Teacher Ideas Press. (800) 237-6124.

Bibliography—Westward Expansion

Nonfiction—Series

The Old West. New York: Time Life Books, varying dates. Grades 6 and up.
Numerous photographs, drawings, maps, and prints are included in these thorough discussions of different aspects of the West. Examples are *The Alaskans, The Forty-niners, The Spanish West, The Pioneers, The Miners, The Ranchers,* and *The Trailblazers.*

Rourke, Arlene, editor. *The Wild West in American History.* Vero Beach, Fla.: Rourke, varying dates. Grades 3 and up.
These colorful, oversized, easy-to-read books provide a good overview of each subject. Examples are *Railroaders* and *Soldiers.*

Nonfiction—Individual Titles

Bloch, Louis M. *Overland to California in 1859: A Guide for Wagon Train Travelers.* Cleveland, Ohio: Bloch and Company, 1990. Grades 4 and up.
Using a variety of sources, such as Randolph B. Marcy's *A Hand-Book for Overland Expeditions,* Bloch has provided the reader with excerpts, maps, and illustrations of sources used for traveling west.

Carlson, Laurie. *Westward Ho! An Activity Guide to the Wild West.* Chicago: Chicago Review Press, 1996. Grades 3 and up.
This resource is packed with an abundance of activities that will enhance any study of the West or westward expansion.

Cobb, Mary. *The Quilt-Block History of Pioneer Days: With Projects Kids Can Make.* Illustrated by Jan Davey Ellis. Brookfield, Conn.: Millbrook Press, 1995. Grades 3 and up.
The contextual history of various types of quilts is described through text and color illustrations. The projects give this an added usefulness.

Cody, Tod. *The Cowboy's Handbook: How to Become a Hero of the Wild West.* New York: Dutton, 1996. Grades 2 and up.
Colorful drawings, illustrations, and diagrams provide youngsters with all the information they need about becoming a cowboy. Includes information on gear, diaries, crafts, cowboy slang, hand signals, and so forth.

Collins, James L. *Exploring the American West.* New York: Franklin Watts, 1989. Grades 3 and up.
Photographs and lithographs illustrate the stories of Daniel Boone, Lewis and Clark, Robert Stuart and Jed Smith, Joseph Reddeford Walker, and John Charles Fremont.

———. *Lawmen of the Old West.* New York: Franklin Watts, 1990. Grades 3 and up.
Key lawmen are described: the town marshall, the sheriff, the United States marshall, and the rangers.

———. *The Mountain Men.* New York: Franklin Watts, 1996. Grades 3 and up.
   Brief biographies and some illustrations are provided for the following: John Colter, Manuel Lisa, Jedediah Strong Smith, Jim Bridger, James P. Beckwourth, Tom "Broken Hand" Fitzpatrick, and Christopher "Kit" Carson.

Erickson, Paul. *Daily Life in a Covered Wagon.* Washington, D.C.: The Preservation Press, 1994. Grades 3 and up.
   This oversized book uses photographs, drawings, and artifacts to provide a fascinating glimpse of what travel was like for those so daring to travel west in a covered wagon.

Fox, Mary Virginia. *The Story of Women Who Shaped the West.* Chicago: Childrens Press, 1991. Grades 2 and up.
   The bravery and motivations of women who helped settle the West are described through text, photographs, and drawings.

Flatley, Dennis R. *The Railroads: Opening the West.* New York: Franklin Watts, 1989. Grades 3 and up.
   Flatley describes the development of the railroad from 1800 to the Civil War with text, black-and-white and color photographs, posters, and maps.

Hewitt, Sally. *The Plains People.* New York: Children's Press, 1996. Grades 1 and up.
   Part of the *Footsteps in Time* series, this book provides activities and introductory information about the Plains Native American Indians.

Kalman, Bobbie, and David Schimpky. *Fort Life.* New York: Crabtree, 1994. Grades 2 and up.
   Bright color photographs of Jamestown, Virginia, provide a glimpse of life that might have been found in a fort as settlers moved west and developed military outposts or fur-trading forts.

Miller, Brandon Marie. *Buffalo Gals: Women of the Old West.* Minneapolis, Minn.: Lerner, 1995. Grades 3 and up.
   Wonderful black-and-white photographs and intriguing text provide insight into the challenges faced by women who moved to the West.

Patent, Dorothy Hinshaw. *West by Covered Wagon: Retracing the Pioneer Trails.* Photographs by William Muñoz. New York: Walker, 1995. Grades 2 and up.
   Join the Westmont Wagoneers as they recreate a wagon train journey through the Flathead Native American Indian Reservation.

Pelz, Ruth. *Women of the Wild West: Biographies from Many Cultures.* Seattle, Wash.: Open Hand, 1995. Grades 3 and up.
   Includes biographies for Sacajawea, Juana Briones de Miranda, Biddy Mason, Mother Joseph (Esther Pariseau), Mary Bong, May Arkwright Hutton, Kate Chapman, and Sarah Winnemucca.

Savage, Jeff. *Pioneering Women of the Wild West.* Springfield, N.J.: Enslow, 1995. Grades 3 and up.
   Savage describes the pivotal roles women played as the West was settled. Part of the Trailblazers of the Wild West series.

————. *Scouts of the Wild West.* Springfield, N.J.: Enslow, 1995. Grades 3 and up.
  Reports of the West from the early scouts encouraged easterners to move westward. Savage describes the efforts of important scouts, such as Kit Carson and Jim Bridger. Part of the Trailblazers of the Wild West series.

Schanzer, Rosalyn. *How We Crossed the West: The Adventures of Lewis and Clark.* Washington, D.C.: National Geographic, 1997. Grades 2 and up.
  Lively illustrations highlight the excerpts from the explorers' journals as they traveled westward in 1804 with Sacagawea.

Schlissel, Lillian. *Black Frontiers: A History of African American Heroes in the Old West.* New York: Simon & Schuster, 1995. Grades 3 and up.
  From mountain men to homesteaders to cowboys to soldiers, Schlissel describes the contributions of black Americans to the settling of the West.

Shapley, Robert W. *Boomtowns.* Illustrated by Luciano Lazzarino. Vero Beach, Fla.: Rourke, 1990. Grades 3 and up.
  Life in the boomtowns of the West is described through text, illustrations, and photographs. Part of the Wild West in American History series.

Steedman, Scott. *A Frontier Fort on the Oregon Trail.* Illustrated by Mark Bergin. New York: Peter Bedrick Books, 1993. Grades 2 and up.
  In addition to describing a frontier fort through text and colorful pictures, the authors describe the Oregon Trail, a pioneer cabin, the building of the railway, a frontier town, the Indian Wars, and the lives of trappers, traders, and Plains Indians.

Stewart, Gail. *Frontiersmen.* Illustrated by Luciano Lazzarino. Vero Beach, Fla.: Rourke, 1990. Grades 3 and up.
  Stewart describes western expansion and those who led the movement. Part of the Wild West in American History series.

Fiction

Anderson, Joan. *Joshua's Westward Journal.* Photographs by George Ancona. New York: William Morrow, 1987. Grades 1 and up.
  Photographed at the Living History Farms in Des Moines, Iowa, this is the story of a family's move west in a Conestoga wagon.

Gilson, Jamie. *Wagon Train 911.* New York: William Morrow, 1996. Grades 4 and up.
  When the fifth grade simulates going west in a wagon train, Dinah resents being paired with Orin. Challenges abound beyond the simulation, but even the failures are celebrated.

Henry, Joanne Landers. *Log Cabin in the Woods: A True Story About a Pioneer Boy.* Illustrated by Joyce Audy Zarins. New York: Macmillan, 1988. All ages.
  Life was challenging, yet never dull for a 12-year-old boy growing up in the Indiana woods. This is a retelling of the true story of Oliver Johnson's early years, as originally told to his grandson, Howard Johnson.

Karr, Kathleen. *Go West, Young Women.* New York: HarperCollins, 1996. Grades 5 and up.

During the trek west, the men in the wagon train suddenly must turn over the leadership to the women. The Petticoat Party wagon train gives a fresh, humorous twist to the history of westward expansion.

———. *Phoebe's Folly.* New York: HarperCollins, 1996. Grades 5 and up.

In this follow-up to *Go West, Young Women,* the wagon train continues its way west, led by the Petticoat Party. Phoebe unwittingly challenges a band of Snake Indians to a shooting and the fun begins!

Levitin, Sonia. *Nine for California.* Illustrated by Cat Bowman Smith. New York: Orchard Books, 1996. Grades kindergarten and up.

When Pa sends for Ma and the family to come west, Ma brings an unusual assortment of items in her sack. Each item saves the day in this fanciful, rollicking tale. The sequel is *Boom Town* (New York: Orchard Books, 1998).

Paul, Ann Whitford. *Eight Hands Round: A Patchwork Alphabet.* Illustrated by Jeanette Winter. New York: HarperCollins, 1991. Grades 1 and up.

The practice of making patchwork quilts is described in this lovely alphabet book. Each type of quilt is described and illustrated.

Sanders, Scott Russell. *Aurora Means Dawn.* Illustrated by Jill Kastner. New York: Bradbury Press, 1989. All ages.

Lovely watercolors enhance this touching story of a family's move to Ohio in the 1800s. Expecting to arrive at a town, not a piece of land, they are nevertheless undaunted and meet the challenge of settling there.

Sandin, Joan. *The Long Way Westward.* New York: Harper and Row, 1989. Grades 1 and up.

This easy-to-read book tells the story of a family who left Sweden and moved from New York to Minnesota.

Shaffer, Ann. *The Camel Express.* Illustrated by Robin Cole. Minneapolis, Minn.: Dillon Press, 1989. Grades 3 and up.

When the Pony Express rider is hurt, Grandpa and Mary Claire ride a camel to the next post.

Turner, Ann. *Dakota Dugout.* New York: Macmillan, 1985. Grades 1 and up.

Life in a sod house is described, including the killing winter, the summer drought, and the unending isolation. Finally the inhabitants' existence improves, but the early years are remembered fondly.

———. *Mississippi Mud: Three Prairie Journals.* Illustrated by Robert J. Blake. New York: HarperCollins, 1997. Grades 2 and up.

Three children describe their family's journey from Kentucky to Oregon. Each viewpoint reflects the unique challenges faced during their travels.

————. *Grasshopper Summer.* New York: Macmillan, 1989. Grades 4 and up.
The Civil War is over and Sem's father wants to make a new life in the Dakota territory. The journey is difficult, the sod house is confining, but the worst is yet to come. Grasshoppers devour the family's long-awaited first harvest.

Van Der Linde, Laurel. *The Pony Express.* New York: Maxwell Macmillan, 1993. Grades 4 and up.
Topics include the early mail routes, the development of the Pony Express, the route, famous rides and riders, the ponies, stations, the Indian War, and the end of the line.

Van Leeuwen, Jean. *Going West.* Illustrated by Thomas B. Allen. New York: Dial, 1992. Grades kindergarten and up.
This simple, elegantly told story describes one family's journey in a covered wagon and their first long winter in their new home.

Van Steenwyk, Elizabeth. *My Name Is York.* Illustrated by Bill Farnsworth. Flagstaff, Ariz.: Northland, 1997. Grades 2 and up.
York, a black slave, accompanies Lewis and Clark on their journey west to find a water passage to the Pacific. On the trip he searches for his own freedom, which is never granted by his owner, Captain Clark.

Wisler, G. Clifton. *Jericho's Journey.* New York: Dutton, 1993. Grades 4 and up.
Jericho's journey to Texas with his family in 1852 presents exciting challenges and unexpected danger.

CD-ROMs

The American Girls Premiere. Minneapolis, Minn.: The Learning Company, 1997. Grades 4 and up.
This multimedia theater production tool, with characters from the American Girls books, includes a focus on pioneering on the Minnesota prairie.

The Westward Movement. Washington, D.C.: National Geographic, 1996. Grades 4 and up.
Meet the explorers, pioneers, and settlers who courageously headed west.

Videos

Heritage of the Black West. Washington, D.C.: National Geographic, 1995. 25 minutes. Grades 4 and up.
Discover the important role of African Americans in the settling of the West.

Tales of the Frontier. Wyoming Public TV. Distributed by Independent Marketing—20/20 Video, 1997. 27 minutes. Grades 4 and up.
Describes life along the Oregon Trail and in the Colorado and Wyoming territories.

5
The Civil War

The Civil War

Word List

- Appomattox
- Blockade runners
- Confederates;
  Carpetbaggers
- Dred Scott Decision
- Exposure
- Food processing
- Gettysburg;
  Grant, Ulysses S.
- Homestead Act
- Icehouse
- Juice
- Kearney, General Philip
- Little Round Top
- Mules
- Naval warfare
- Oil
- Profiteers
- Quantrill, William C.
- Railroads
- Sherman, William T.
- Transportation
- Underground railroad
- Vegetable preservation
- Wagons
- X
- Yankees
- Zoaves

A Soldier's Ration

A soldier's daily camp ration:

> 12 ounces of pork or bacon or 20 ounces salt or fresh beef
> 22 ounces soft bread or flour or 16 ounces hard bread or 20 ounces cornmeal

With every hundred such rations, there should be:

> 1 peck of beans or peas
> 10 pounds of rice or hominy
> 10 pounds of green coffee or 8 pounds of roasted and ground coffee or 1½ pounds of tea
> 15 pounds of sugar
> 20 ounces of candles
> 4 pounds of soap
> 2 quarts of salt
> 4 quarts of vinegar
> 4 ounces pepper
> ½ bushel potatoes
> 1 quart molasses

Marching ration:

> 1 pound hard bread
> ¾ pound salt pork or 1 ¼ pound fresh meat
> Sugar
> Coffee
> Salt

Source: Billings, John D. *Hardtack and Coffee: The Unwritten Story of Army Life.* Illustrated by Charles W. Reed. Boston: George M. Smith and Company, 1887.

BUTTERMILK PANCAKES

Ingredients

1 cup flour
2 teaspoons sugar
½ teaspoon salt
½ teaspoon baking powder
½ teaspoon baking soda

1 egg
2 tablespoons melted butter
1 cup buttermilk or sour milk*
1 tablespoon shortening
Butter and maple syrup

Steps

1. Mix flour, sugar, salt, baking powder, and baking soda together in a large bowl.
2. Beat egg in a small bowl. Add melted butter and milk. Mix well.
3. Pour liquid mixture into dry mixture and stir only long enough to wet the dry ingredients. Do not overbeat.
4. Heat a griddle over medium heat or heat electric griddle to medium setting.
5. Melt 1 tablespoon of shortening on griddle.
6. Drop batter onto hot griddle.
7. When holes or bubbles appear evenly on the top of each pancake, turn it over.
8. Cook until brown on both sides.
9. Serve hot with butter and maple syrup.

*To sour milk, add 1 tablespoon vinegar or lemon juice to milk and let stand for 10 minutes to curdle.

Makes 10 to 12 pancakes.

DOUGH NUTS

Ingredients

4 tablespoons butter
½ cup sugar
2 eggs
¼ teaspoon salt
½ teaspoon cinnamon

1 teaspoon baking powder
2 ½ cups flour
Oil for frying
Sugar for sprinkling over cooked dough
    nuts

Steps

1. Cream butter and sugar together.
2. Beat in eggs.
3. Stir in salt, cinnamon, and baking powder.
4. Stir in enough of the flour to form a stiff dough, then turn dough out onto table and knead in the rest of the flour.
5. Heat about 3 inches of oil in a heavy pan.
6. Roll dough into balls about 1 ½ inches wide.
7. Drop balls into hot fat and cook until brown on all sides.
8. Remove balls from hot fat with a slotted spoon and drain on paper towels.
9. Sprinkle sugar over each dough nut.

Makes 8 to 12.

From *Cooking Up U.S. History*, Second Edition. © 1999 Suzanne I. Barchers and Patricia C. Marden. Teacher Ideas Press. (800) 237-6124.

FRIED POTATOES

Ingredients
Potatoes
Butter for frying
Salt, to taste

Steps
1. Peel potatoes.
2. Cut potatoes into thin slices.
3. Melt butter in frying pan over medium heat.
4. Add potato slices to pan and fry until brown on both sides.
5. Add salt to taste.

HARDTACK

Ingredients
3 cups flour
2 teaspoons salt
1 cup water

Steps
1. In a large bowl, mix flour and salt.
2. Add water and stir or work with hands to blend.
3. Knead dough, adding more flour if mixture becomes sticky. Turn out onto a floured board.
4. Roll the dough into a rectangle ½-inch thick.
5. Using a sharp knife, cut the dough into 3-inch squares.
6. Using a large nail, poke 16 holes through each square.
7. Bake at 375 degrees for 25 minutes or until brown.
8. Store in an airtight container.

Makes 12.

BEATEN BISCUITS

Ingredients

4 cups flour
1 ¼ teaspoons salt
2 teaspoons sugar
4 tablespoons lard or 5 tablespoons
     softened margarine

½ cup cold milk
½ cup cold water
Melted butter

Steps

1.   Mix flour, salt, and sugar well in a large bowl.
2.   Work lard into the dry ingredients with a pastry blender or with hands.
3.   Slowly add the milk and water, stirring constantly until it forms a soft dough. Use your hands, but do not over mix.
4.   Place a clean linen towel on the table and sprinkle with flour.
5.   Place the dough on the towel and beat with a wooden mallet or rolling pin until it is flattened.
6.   Fold the sides up to the center and beat until flattened again.
7.   Continue beating and folding for 20 minutes.
8.   During the last beating, beat to about 1-inch high and cut out with round cutter dipped in flour.
9.   Poke top of biscuits with a fork and brush with melted butter.
10.   Bake at 350 degrees for 25 minutes or until browned.

Makes 10.

ARMY BREAD

Ingredients

1 package yeast
1 cup very warm water
1 cup flour

2 cups warm water
2 ½ teaspoons salt
Flour

Steps

1.   Mix yeast, 1 cup very warm water, and 1 cup flour in a medium bowl. Stir well. Let sit at room temperature overnight.
2.   Place mixture in a very large bowl. Add remaining ingredients. Add enough flour to make a soft dough.
3.   Place dough on a floured board. Knead until smooth and elastic.
4.   Grease bowl. Place dough in bowl.
5.   Let rise in a warm place until double in size.
6.   Punch dough down. Let rise again until double in size.
7.   Divide dough into 3 equal pieces.
8.   Put into greased loaf pans.
9.   Let rise in warm place until double in size.
10.   Bake in a 375 degree oven 40 to 60 minutes until done.

Makes 3 loaves.

CHICKEN PIE

Ingredients

Crust
⅔ cup shortening
2 cups flour
½ teaspoon salt
¼ cup cold water

Filling
3 cups cooked chicken, cut into bite-size pieces
2 slices raw bacon
⅓ cup flour
2 eggs
1 cup chicken broth
Salt and pepper (to taste)

Steps

1. Mix shortening into flour and salt with a pastry blender or hands.
2. Sprinkle with cold water and toss with a fork until dough forms a ball. Do not add more water than necessary and do not over mix.
3. Divide dough into 2 equal parts.
4. Roll 1 part into a 12-inch circle.
5. Line a 9-inch pie pan with the dough. Trim the edge to 1 inch wider than the pan.
6. Sprinkle the cooked chicken evenly over the bottom of the crust.
7. Cut bacon into small pieces and sprinkle over the chicken.
8. Sprinkle ⅓ cup of flour over chicken and bacon.
9. Beat eggs in a small bowl.
10. Beat chicken broth into eggs.
11. Pour liquid mixture over the chicken mixture.
12. Salt and pepper to taste.
13. Roll second part of dough into a 12-inch circle.
14. Cover pie with dough, folding under and sealing edges.
15. Use a knife to put 3 slashes about 1 inch long in the top crust.
16. Bake in a 375 degree oven for 45 minutes or until browned and bubbly.

Makes 1 9-inch pie.

From *Cooking Up U.S. History*, Second Edition. © 1999 Suzanne I. Barchers and Patricia C. Marden. Teacher Ideas Press. (800) 237-6124.

SPONGE CAKE

Ingredients
6 eggs, separated
¼ teaspoon salt
2 cups sugar
2 ¼ cups flour

Steps
1. Beat egg whites until stiff.
2. Beat in salt.
3. Beat egg yolks in a separate bowl.
4. Slowly add sugar to egg yolks while beating.
5. Continue beating until thick and lemon colored.
6. Gently fold yolk mixture into egg white mixture.
7. Gently fold flour into mixture.
8. Grease and flour a 9-inch tube pan.
9. Carefully spoon batter into pan.
10. Bake at 375 degrees for 1 hour or until done.

Makes 1 cake.

GINGERBREAD

Ingredients
½ cup softened butter or margarine
½ cup sugar
¾ cup molasses
2 eggs
1 tablespoon ginger
1 ½ teaspoons cinnamon
2 ½ teaspoons baking soda
¾ cup boiling water
2 ¾ cups flour

Steps
1. Cream butter or margarine.
2. Stir sugar, molasses, and eggs into butter.
3. Stir in ginger, cinnamon, and baking soda.
4. Stir in half of the water, then half of the flour.
5. Stir in the rest of the water, then the rest of the flour.
6. Grease a 9-by-13-inch baking pan.
7. Pour batter into the pan and bake at 350 degrees for 25 minutes or until center springs back when touched lightly.

Serves 16.

From *Cooking Up U.S. History*, Second Edition. © 1999 Suzanne I. Barchers and Patricia C. Marden. Teacher Ideas Press. (800) 237-6124.

HOE CAKE

Ingredients
1 cup cornmeal
½ teaspoon salt
1 ½ tablespoons oil
1 cup boiling water
Butter or jam

Steps
1. Put cornmeal and salt in a medium bowl. Stir together.
2. Add the oil and half of the water. Stir well.
3. Add the rest of the water. Work it in with your hands.
4. Grease a cookie sheet.
5. Divide the dough into thirds and shape it into 3 round, flat shapes on the cookie sheet.
6. Bake in a 375 degree oven for about 30 minutes or until browned.
7. Serve warm with butter or jam.

Serves 4.

APPLEADE

Ingredients
2 large apples
1 quart water
Sugar (to taste)

Steps
1. Core and cut apples into slices. Do not peel. Place in a pan.
2. Boil the water.
3. Pour boiling water over apple slices.
4. Let mixture sit for 30 minutes.
5. Strain well.
6. Sweeten to taste with sugar.
7. Chill.

Serves 6.

HOT CHOCOLATE

Ingredients
1 ½ cups water
1 ounce unsweetened chocolate
¼ cup sugar
2 ¼ cups milk

Steps
1. Put water in a medium saucepan and bring to a boil over medium high heat.
2. Turn heat down to medium low and add chocolate. Stir until chocolate melts.
3. Add sugar and stir until dissolved.
4. Stir in milk.
5. Serve hot.

Serves 4.

BARLEY WATER

Ingredients
½ cup barley
3 pints water
Peel of 1 lemon
Sugar (to taste)

Steps
1. Put barley, water, and lemon peel in a saucepan.
2. Simmer for 30 to 45 minutes.
3. Add sugar to taste.
4. Strain and drink while hot.

Serves 6.

Library Links

Library Link 1:   Who was Gail Borden? What important role did he play during the Civil War?

Library Link 2:   The dough nuts during this period did not have holes. When were holes added to what we now call "doughnuts"?

Library Link 3:   Where did potatoes originate? How did they get to North America?

Library Link 4:   Hardtack was a staple of Civil War soldiers. It was often infested with weevils. What are weevils?

Library Link 5:   What effect did the passing of the Homestead Act have on farming?

Library Link 6:   Research the contrast between food production in the North and in the South during the Civil War.

Library Link 7:   What effect did Sherman's march to the sea have on the food supplies of the South?

Library Link 8:   Where did ginger come from?

Library Link 9:   How did hoe cake get its name?

Library Link 10:   Approximately how much did a barrel of apple cider cost during the Civil War?

Library Link 11:   How was the cacao bean prepared for a chocolate drink?

Library Link 12:   The Civil War soldiers loved coffee, but often substituted grains for coffee. What else did they use to make coffee substitutes?

From *Cooking Up U.S. History*, Second Edition. © 1999 Suzanne I. Barchers and Patricia C. Marden. Teacher Ideas Press. (800) 237-6124.

Bibliography—The Civil War

Nonfiction

Ashabranner, Brent. *A Memorial for Mr. Lincoln.* Photographs by Jennifer Ashabranner. New York: G. P. Putnam's Sons, 1992. Grades 4 and up.
   The history of the building of the memorial is interspersed with anecdotes and photographs. The historical photographs, such as that of 250,000 people waiting to hear Dr. Martin Luther King Jr. speak in 1963, make this an intriguing book.

Bial, Raymond. *Where Lincoln Walked.* New York: Walker, 1997. Grades 3 and up.
   Focusing on Lincoln's early years, the rich photographs enhance a fascinating overview of Lincoln's homes, schooling, and family life.

Bolotin, Norman, and Angela Herb. *For Home and Country: A Civil War Scrapbook.* New York: Dutton, 1995. Grades 4 and up.
   This extensive resource includes a variety of enhancements to the text: photographs, art, letters, artifacts, and a time line. The glossary and bibliography are useful touches.

Carter, Alden R. *Battle of the Ironclads: The Monitor and the Merrimack.* New York: Franklin Watts, 1993. Grades 4 and up.
   This famous battle is described with text, photographs of key figures, and drawings of the events.

Chang, Ina. *A Separate Battle: Women and the Civil War.* New York: Dutton, 1991. Grades 5 and up.
   This resource fills a gap in history—the role of women in the Civil War. Their work as nurses, spies, abolitionists, and even as disguised soldiers proves inspirational for all readers.

Damon, Duane. *When This Cruel War Is Over: The Civil War Home Front.* Minneapolis, Minn.: Lerner, 1996. Grades 5 and up.
   Enriched by photographs and drawings, Damon's text describes the effect of the war on Americans' homes and individual lives.

Freedman, Russell. *Lincoln: A Photobiography.* New York: Scholastic Book, 1987. Grades 4 and up.
   Photographs, posters, portraits, and text provide an enlightening biography of Lincoln. This is a Newbery Medal book.

Kent, Zachary. *The Battle of Antietam.* Chicago: Childrens Press, 1992. Grades 3 and up.
   The horror of this devastating battle is described with matter-of-fact text, photographs, and drawings.

Kunhardt, Edith. *Honest Abe.* Illustrated by Malcah Zeldis. New York: Greenwillow, 1993. All ages.
   This simple recounting of Abraham Lincoln's life has bright illustrations. The Gettysburg Address is included, along with a time line of significant events in his life.

From *Cooking Up U.S. History*, Second Edition. © 1999 Suzanne I. Barchers and Patricia C. Marden. Teacher Ideas Press. (800) 237-6124.

Lincoln, Abraham. *The Gettysburg Address.* Illustrated by Michael McCurdy. Boston: Houghton Mifflin, 1995. Grades 4 and up.
This inspiring speech is beautifully illustrated with black and white line drawings.

Marrin, Albert. *Unconditional Surrender: U.S. Grant and the Civil War.* New York: Atheneum, 1994. Grades 6 and up.
Marrin recounts Ulysses S. Grant's efforts to end the war, including descriptions of the soldiers' living conditions, the horrors of the war, and Grant's eventual success.

Meltzer, Milton, editor. *Lincoln, In His Own Words.* Illustrated by Stephen Alcorn. San Diego, Calif.: Harcourt Brace and Company, 1993. Grades 5 and up.
Drawing upon his speeches, letters, and writings, Meltzer has compiled a fascinating representation of Lincoln's dedication to the country.

Murphy, Jim. *The Boys' War: Confederate and Union Soldiers Talk About the Civil War.* New York: Clarion Books, 1990. Grades 5 and up.
Going to war seemed a romantic notion to youngsters. Drawing from first-hand accounts and photographs, Murphy provides a chilling glimpse into the realities of war for these children.

Ray, Delia. *Behind the Blue and Gray: The Soldier's Life in the Civil War.* New York: Dutton, 1991. Grades 5 and up.
This sequel to *A Nation Torn: The Story of How the Civil War Began* details the hardships of the war and how the soldiers coped with poor conditions, disease, and death. Photographs, art, and drawings enhance the resource.

———. *A Nation Torn: The Story of How the Civil War Began.* New York: Penguin, 1990. Grades 5 and up.
Using primary resources, Ray provides a detailed discussion of the events leading up to the Civil War.

Reef, Catherine. *Civil War Soldiers.* New York: Holt, 1993. Grades 4 and up.
Reef describes the role of black soldiers in the Civil War. Includes a chronology, bibliography, and index.

Sandler, Martin W. *Civil War.* New York: HarperCollins, 1996. Grades 4 and up.
Drawn from the resources of the Library of Congress, the many photographs plus the quotes from primary sources make this resource a necessity for any study of the Civil War.

Fiction

Armstrong, Jennifer. *The Dreams of Mairhe Mehan.* New York: Alfred A. Knopf, 1996. Grades 5 and up. Preread.
Mairhe, a young Irish woman, lives in the slums of Washington, D.C., during the Civil War. Her father's self-destruction and her brother's departure and death in the war make up this realistic and tragic story.

Bunting, Eve. *The Blue and the Gray.* New York: Scholastic, 1996. All ages.
 Two young boys discuss the Civil War battleground that their new houses are being built on, speculating on the lives and friendships lost.

Denenberg, Barry. *When Will This Cruel War Be Over? The Civil War Diary of Emma Simpson.* New York: Scholastic, 1996. Grades 5 and up.
 A young girl keeps a diary during the tragic years of the Civil War. Her voice lends authenticity to the impact the war had on individual lives.

Fleischman, Paul. *Bull Run.* New York: HarperCollins, 1993. Grades 4 and up.
 Told through multiple voices, this powerful recreation of the battle at Bull Run can be read as a novel or as readers' theater. Often moving, this should be considered for any study of the Civil War.

Forrester, Sandra. *Sound the Jubilee.* New York: Dutton, 1995. Grades 5 and up.
 The Civil War has begun and the slaves at River Bend Plantation are anxious for freedom to arrive. When the Yankees turn Roanoke Island into a refuge for runaway slaves, Maddie and her family face the possibility and risks of freedom.

Fritz, Jean. *Stonewall.* New York: Putnam, 1979, 1997. Grades 5 and up.
 From his humble beginnings to his struggles at West Point, Thomas Jackson dedicated himself to achieving greatness. As a heroic soldier, he found his strength, demonstrating that he could be an outstanding military leader.

Hamilton, Virginia. *Many Thousand Gone: African Americans from Slavery to Freedom.* Illustrated by Leo and Diane Dillon. New York: Alfred A. Knopf, 1993. Grades 4 and up.
 Hamilton profiles key events and people in the history of America. Beginning with information about slavery, she moves through the years of escape and finally the years of exodus to freedom.

Polacco, Patricia. *Pink and Say.* New York: Philomel Books, 1994. Grades 3 and up.
 Pinkus, a black soldier with the Union, discovers and rescues a young, injured, white Union soldier. Pinkus carries the soldier to his mother, who nurses him faithfully. The youngster confesses that he was deserting when injured but is reassured that he is not a coward, only young. Tragedy strikes, and the friends are taken to the prison at Andersonville, where only one survives.

Reeder, Carolyn. *Shades of Gray.* New York: Macmillan, 1989. Grades 4 and up.
 Will Page has lost his family to the Civil War, and now he must live with his Uncle Jed, who refused to fight the hated Yankees. Will must come to grips with his growing respect for Uncle Jed while resenting his noninvolvement with the war.

Seymour, Tres. *We Played Marbles.* Illustrated by Dan Andreasen. New York: Orchard Books, 1998. Grades kindergarten and up.
 Two boys play soldiers on a Civil War site until Papaw suggests they play marbles instead.

Stolz, Mary. *A Ballad of the Civil War.* New York: HarperCollins, 1997. Grades 3 and up.
 Inspired by a ballad, Stolz has written a story of twin brothers who choose different sides during the Civil War.

Winnick, Karen B. *Mr. Lincoln's Whiskers.* Honesdale, Pa.: Boyds Mills Press, 1996. Grades 1 and up.

Grace Bedell decides that Mr. Lincoln would look less sad with whiskers and writes her suggestion to him. Reproductions of the actual letters are included in the back of the book.

Wisler, G. Clifton. *Mr. Lincoln's Drummer.* New York: Penguin, 1995. Grades 5 and up.

Willie joins the army as a drummer and is given the rare privilege of drumming for Mr. Lincoln. Pair this story of Willie's challenges with the previously mentioned Jim Murphy's *The Boys' War: Confederate and Union Soldiers Talk About the Civil War.*

———. *Red Cap.* New York: Dutton, 1991. Grades 4 and up.

When Ransom J. Powell joins the Union army, he becomes a drummer boy. But this doesn't prevent his being captured and taken to a prison at Andersonville, Georgia.

CD-ROMs

The American Girls Premiere. Minneapolis, Minn.: The Learning Company, 1997. Grades 4 and up.

This multimedia theater production tool with characters from the American Girls books includes a focus on the Civil War.

The Civil War. Washington, D.C.: National Geographic, 1997. Grades 4 and up.

From the beginning of the war through Lee's surrender, this book examines the reasons for and effects of the war.

Kits

National Archives and Jean West. *The Civil War: A Survey.* Peterborough, N.H.: Cobblestone, n.d. Grades 4 and up.

This kit includes 42 documents and 30 lessons for teaching with primary sources.

Who Was Abraham Lincoln? Washington, D.C.: National Geographic, 1993. Grades Kindergarten to 2.

Kit includes a cassette, student booklets, reproducibles, library catalog cards, and teacher's guide.

6
The Northeast

Maine

Vt.

N.H.

Mass.

Conn.

R.I.

The Northeast

Word List

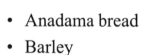

- Anadama bread
- Barley
- Cobbler, Corn oysters, Clambakes
- Duck
- Eggs
- Flummery, Fish fries
- Grunts
- Hasty pudding
- Indian pudding
- Johnnycake
- *Kedgeree*
- Love apples
- Marsh rubies, Mincemeat

- New England boiled dinner
- Oysters
- Pandowdy
- Quahog
- Red flannel hash
- Slumps, Sugar on the snow parties, Snickerdoodles
- Turkey
- Umbelliferae
- Vermont apple pie
- Wine
- X
- Yankee pumpkin pudding
- Zabaglione

BLUEBERRY MUFFINS

Ingredients
2 cups flour
½ cup sugar
2 tablespoons baking powder
1 teaspoon baking soda
½ teaspoon salt
2 eggs
1 cup sour milk* or buttermilk
¼ cup butter, melted
1 tablespoon flour
1 cup blueberries

Steps
1. Preheat oven to 400 degrees.
2. Grease 12 muffin cups or use cupcake papers.
3. Mix together flour, sugar, baking powder, baking soda, and salt in a large mixing bowl.
4. In a small bowl mix together eggs, sour milk, and melted butter.
5. Stir liquid ingredients into dry ingredients. Mix only until dry ingredients are moistened. Do not overmix.
6. In a small bowl stir 1 tablespoon flour into blueberries.
7. Gently stir blueberries into dough.
8. Pour batter into muffin tins.
9. Bake 20 minutes or until light brown on top.
10. Serve hot with butter.

*To sour milk, stir 1 tablespoon vinegar or lemon juice into 1 cup of milk and let stand 10 minutes to curdle.

Makes 12.

FRIED DOUGH

Ingredients
1 ½ cups flour
1 ¼ teaspoons baking powder
¾ teaspoon salt
2 tablespoons lard or shortening, softened
½ cup warm water
Oil for frying
Optional: tomato sauce, cinnamon sugar, confectioner's sugar

Steps
1.   Mix flour, baking powder, and salt.
2.   Cut in shortening until mixture begins to form small balls of dough.
3.   Stir in warm water.
4.   Turn dough out onto a floured board and knead for 2 to 3 minutes.
5.   Cover dough with a towel and let it rest for about 15 minutes.
6.   Heat about ¼ inch of oil in a large frying pan to 375 degrees.
7.   Divide dough into 5 equal pieces.
8.   Roll each piece into a ball. Then flatten into a 5-inch circle.
9.   Using a sharp knife, cut 4 1-inch slits into dough.
10.   Place circles of dough carefully into hot oil.
11.   Cook until brown and then turn and brown on other side.
12.   Drain on paper towels.
13.   Serve immediately with tomato sauce, cinnamon sugar, or confectioner's sugar.

Makes 5.

RAISED DOUGHNUTS

Ingredients

1 package dry yeast
1 tablespoon sugar
2 tablespoons very warm water (110 to 115 degrees)
½ cup sugar
1 egg, beaten
1 cup milk
3 tablespoons melted butter
3 ½ to 4 cups flour
Oil for frying
Butter for greasing

Steps

1. Combine yeast, 1 tablespoon sugar, and warm water in small bowl. Stir until all yeast is dissolved.
2. Let yeast mixture stand 10 to 15 minutes or until foamy.
3. Mix ½ cup sugar, egg, milk, and melted butter in a large bowl.
4. Add yeast mixture to egg mixture and mix well.
5. Stir in 3 ½ cups flour to form a soft dough.
6. Add more flour if dough is too sticky.
7. Grease a large bowl and put dough in it.
8. Brush top with melted butter.
9. Cover bowl with plastic wrap and let rise in warm place until doubled in size.
10. Divide dough in half.
11. Roll ½ of dough out on floured board to about ½ inch thick.
12. Cut out doughnuts with a 2- to 3-inch doughnut cutter.
13. Place cut doughnuts on floured board and cover with a towel.
14. Repeat with the other half of dough.
15. Let dough rise again until doubled in size.
16. In a deep fryer heat at least 3 inches of oil until it reaches 375 degrees. Keep oil at this temperature.
17. Place doughnuts in oil and fry until browned on both sides.
18. Remove from oil and drain on paper towels.
19. Eat while warm. After they are cool, they are very dry. Try dunking them in milk, coffee, or maple syrup.

Makes 12 to 15.

STEAMED CLAMS

Ingredients
5 dozen clams (littleneck or cherrystone)
Water
½ teaspoon salt
¼ pound butter

Steps
1. Rinse clams in cold water twice to remove sand and grit.
2. Pour about ½ inch of water into a large kettle.
3. Add salt and clams. Cover kettle.
4. Bring water to a boil and simmer about 10 minutes until clams open.
5. Remove clams from liquid and throw away any that did not open. Liquid may be saved and used as clam broth in other recipes.
6. Melt butter.
7. Remove clams from shells with a fork, dip in melted butter, and eat.

Serves 5.

FRIED CLAMS

Ingredients
¾ cup milk
¾ cup evaporated milk
1 large egg
¾ teaspoon vanilla
¼ teaspoon salt
Dash of pepper
4 ½ dozen clams, removed from shell (littleneck, cherrystone, or Ipswich)
⅔ cup flour
1 ⅔ cups cornmeal
Oil for frying

Steps
1. Combine milk, evaporated milk, egg, vanilla, salt, and pepper.
2. Clams may be kept whole or cut into smaller pieces.
3. Soak clams in milk mixture.
4. Combine flour and cornmeal in a small bowl.
5. Drop clams into flour and cornmeal mixture and turn until coated.
6. Heat oil to 375 degrees.
7. Fry clams in oil until browned on both sides.
8. Drain on paper towels.
9. Serve immediately.

Serves 5.

BOILED LOBSTER

Ingredients
2 gallons water
¼ cup salt
4 bay leaves
4 live lobsters, 1 ½ to 2 pounds each
1 stick butter

Steps
1. Pour water into a large kettle or lobster pot.
2. Add the salt and bay leaves.
3. Bring water to boil.
4. Drop lobsters into boiling water. Cover with lid.
5. Lower heat to simmer. Boil for 10 minutes.
6. Put butter in a small saucepan over low heat and melt, or melt the butter in the microwave.
7. Remove lobsters from water and crack shells.
8. Serve by removing from shell and dipping in melted butter.

Serves 4.

CORN OYSTERS

Ingredients
1 large egg
1 cup whole-kernel corn
½ teaspoon salt
¼ teaspoon pepper
⅓ cup flour
2 tablespoons milk
Oil for frying

Steps
1. Beat egg in medium-size bowl.
2. Drain corn and add to egg.
3. Stir in salt, pepper, flour, and milk until mixture is well combined.
4. Pour oil about ¼ inch deep in a large frying pan.
5. Heat oil over medium heat.
6. Drop corn mixture by tablespoons into hot oil.
7. Fry until brown on bottom. Turn over and brown other side.
8. Serve as a vegetable or main dish with maple syrup.

Makes 10 to 12.

From *Cooking Up U.S. History*, Second Edition. © 1999 Suzanne I. Barchers and Patricia C. Marden. Teacher Ideas Press. (800) 237-6124.

RED FLANNEL HASH

Ingredients

3 medium potatoes
3 tablespoons butter
1 12-ounce can corned beef, chopped
1 1-pound can sliced beets, chopped

¼ cup chopped onion
½ cup cream
Salt and pepper (to taste)

Steps

1. Boil potatoes until soft and then chop into small cubes.
2. Melt butter in a large frying pan over medium heat.
3. Put beef, beets, potatoes, and onion in frying pan and saute until browned.
4. Pour cream over mixture.
5. Cook for about 15 minutes or until a brown crust forms around the edges of the pan.
6. Add salt and pepper to taste.

Serves 4 to 5.

NEW ENGLAND CLAM CHOWDER

Ingredients

8 ounces chopped clams in clam juice
4 strips bacon
1 small onion
2 large potatoes
½ teaspoon salt

¼ teaspoon pepper
1 ½ cups milk
⅓ cup light cream
1 ½ tablespoons milk
1 tablespoon flour

Steps

1. Drain clams and save juice.
2. Cook the bacon in a large saucepan over medium-high heat until crisp.
3. Drain bacon on paper towel.
4. Chop onion.
5. Add onion to bacon grease and cook until clear.
6. Peel potatoes and chop into small cubes.
7. Add potatoes to onion.
8. Pour clam juice into a measuring cup and add water until it equals 1 cup.
9. Add clam juice to saucepan with potatoes and onions and cook over medium heat until potatoes are tender.
10. Add salt, pepper, 1 ½ cups milk, and light cream to saucepan.
11. Add the 1 ½ tablespoons of milk to the 1 tablespoon of flour in a small bowl and stir until well mixed.
12. Slowly stir the flour mixture into the saucepan and turn heat to medium-high. Keep stirring until the mixture just starts to boil.
13. Remove from heat immediately.
14. Taste and add more salt and pepper if desired.
15. When reheating chowder, do not boil.

Serves 6.

From *Cooking Up U.S. History*, Second Edition. © 1999 Suzanne I. Barchers and Patricia C. Marden. Teacher Ideas Press. (800) 237-6124.

HARVARD BEETS

Ingredients
8 large beets
⅔ cup sugar
2 teaspoons cornstarch
⅓ cup water
¼ cup vinegar
4 tablespoons butter
Salt and pepper (to taste)

Steps
1. Peel beets and cook in boiling water until tender.
2. Cool beets and cut into slices about ¼ inch thick.
3. Mix sugar and cornstarch.
4. Add sugar and cornstarch to water and mix well.
5. Pour mixture into a saucepan and add vinegar.
6. Boil over medium-high heat for 5 minutes.
7. Add beets, stir, and let stand 30 minutes to 1 hour with heat off.
8. To serve, bring to a boil and stir in butter, salt, and pepper.

Serves 6.

CRANBERRY SAUCE

Ingredients
1 pound cranberries
2 ½ cups sugar
½ cup molasses or maple syrup

Steps
1. Wash cranberries and remove stems.
2. Put cranberries in saucepan and add about ½ inch of water.
3. Bring to a boil and simmer over low heat about 15 minutes, until cranberries are soft.
4. Stir sugar and molasses into hot sauce and remove from heat.
5. May be served hot or cold.

Serves 8.

From *Cooking Up U.S. History*, Second Edition. © 1999 Suzanne I. Barchers and Patricia C. Marden. Teacher Ideas Press. (800) 237-6124.

APPLE PANDOWDY

Ingredients

Pastry

1 cup flour
½ teaspoon salt

¼ cup shortening, softened
¼ cup cold water

Filling

8 large apples
½ cup sugar
½ teaspoon cinnamon
½ teaspoon nutmeg
⅛ teaspoon cloves
⅛ teaspoon salt

⅓ cup molasses
Water
3 tablespoons melted butter
3 tablespoons molasses
Cream

Steps

Pastry

1. Mix flour and salt.
2. Cut in shortening with a pastry blender.
3. Add water and stir lightly until dough pulls away from sides of bowl.
4. Put dough onto a floured board.
5. Pat out into a small square.
6. Cut off ⅔ of the dough and roll into a strip about 3 inches wide and 25 inches long.
7. Arrange strip to fit around the inside wall of a 1 ½ quart casserole dish. Do not cover the bottom of the dish. Make sure pastry is about ½ inch higher than the edge of the casserole dish.
8. Preheat oven to 425 degrees.

Filling

1. Peel, core, and cut apples into quarters.
2. In a large bowl, combine apples, sugar, cinnamon, nutmeg, cloves, and salt.
3. Measure the ⅓ cup molasses and add enough water to make ½ cup.
4. Add molasses mixture to apple mixture.
5. Stir in melted butter.
6. Pour apple mixture into casserole dish.
7. Roll out the rest of the pastry so that it is a little bit larger than the top of the casserole dish.
8. Place pastry on top of apple mixture and press top pastry to side pastry, tucking in edges around the inside of the dish.
9. Bake at 425 degrees for 20 to 25 minutes or until crust is light brown.
10. Remove from oven.
11. Turn oven down to 350 degrees.
12. Take 2 knives and cut crust into pieces by crisscrossing the crust.
13. Cover casserole dish and put it back in the oven for 20 more minutes.
14. Remove dish from oven, uncover, and drizzle 3 tablespoons molasses over the top.
15. Bake uncovered for 10 more minutes.
16. Serve warm with or without cream.

Serves 8.

BUTTERNUT CAKE

Ingredients

Cake
½ cup butter, softened
⅓ cup sugar
1 cup maple syrup
2 eggs
2 ½ cups flour
1 ¾ teaspoons baking powder
½ teaspoon baking soda
¼ teaspoon ginger
½ cup hot water
½ cup butternut meats, chopped

Frosting
2 cups maple syrup
¼ teaspoon salt
1 cup light cream
½ cup butternut meats, finely chopped

Steps

1. Preheat oven to 350 degrees.
2. Cream butter and sugar together in large bowl.
3. Add syrup and beat well.
4. Add eggs and beat well.
5. In medium bowl, mix together flour, baking powder, baking soda, and ginger.
6. Add half of the dry ingredients to butter mixture and mix well.
7. Add half of the hot water to butter mixture and mix well.
8. Add rest of dry ingredients and rest of hot water, mixing well after each addition.
9. Stir in butternut meats.
10. Grease a loaf pan.
11. Pour batter in pan and bake for 45 minutes. When done, toothpick inserted in center should come out clean.
12. For frosting, put maple syrup, salt, and cream in medium saucepan.
13. Cook over medium-high heat until mixture boils, stirring constantly.
14. Continue boiling until it reaches the soft-ball stage, forming a soft ball when a bit is dropped into a cup of cold water.
15. Add nuts. Beat until creamy and thick enough to spread.
16. Spread on cooled cake.

Serves 6 to 8.

PUMPKIN PIE

Ingredients
1 9-inch pie shell
1 small cooking pumpkin
3 eggs
1 ¾ cups evaporated milk
½ cup molasses
¼ cup sugar
¼ teaspoon salt
2 tablespoons cinnamon
1 tablespoon ginger
½ teaspoon cloves
½ teaspoon allspice

Steps
1. Cut pumpkin into about 8 small chunks.
2. Peel off outside skin.
3. Remove seeds.
4. Simmer in a saucepan with water until pumpkin is tender. Drain.
5. Force pumpkin through a food mill.
6. Use 2 to 2 ½ cups of strained pumpkin for pie. The rest may be frozen for another use.
7. Beat eggs in a large bowl.
8. Add pumpkin, milk, molasses, sugar, salt, cinnamon, ginger, cloves, and allspice. Stir well.
9. Pour pumpkin mixture into pie shell.
10. Bake in a 400 degree oven for 15 minutes.
11. Turn oven down to 375 degrees and cook for 30 more minutes or until a knife inserted in the center comes out clean.

Serves 8.

Library Links

Library Link 1:   Find out what a bilberry is.

Library Link 2:   When did good-quality wheat flour become readily available?

Library Link 3:   Today we often fry in melted shortening or vegetable oil. What did the early settlers use for frying?

Library Link 4:   A clam is a bivalved mollusk. What does bivalved mean?

Library Link 5:   Which type of clam is larger, littleneck or cherrystone?

Library Link 6:   Corn oysters were given their name because they are shaped like oysters. A similar name is given to a very different food, the coon oyster. Find out what coon oysters are and how they got their name.

Library Link 7:   What are other meanings for the word *hash*?

Library Link 8:   Identify as many types of clams as you can.

Library Link 9:   What part of the beet plant is eaten?

Library Link 10:   How did cranberries get their name?

Library Link 11:   Find the meaning of the word *pandowdy.*

Library Link 12:   Why did the Native American Indians plant pumpkin with corn?

Bibliography—The Northeast

Nonfiction

Gemming, Elizabeth. *The Cranberry Book.* New York: Coward-McCann, 1983. Grades 4 and up.
  Gemming describes the contribution of cranberries to the diet of the colonists, as well as their cultivation and harvesting.

Harness, Cheryl. *The Amazing Impossible Erie Canal.* New York: Macmillan Books for Young Readers, 1995. Grades 2 and up.
  Connecting Lake Erie to the Atlantic Ocean seemed an overwhelming undertaking, but Americans in the early 1800s recognized that a canal would be a wise investment. This lively description details the digging of the 363-mile-long canal, the longest in the world.

Weinstein-Farson, Laurie. *Indians of North America: The Wampanoag.* New York: Chelsea House, 1989. Grades 4 and up.
  The 200-year struggle and survival of this tribe that lived along the shores of Cape Cod is described with text and a variety of photographs.

Fiction

Cooney, Barbara. *Island Boy.* New York: Viking Penguin, 1988. All ages.
  Matthais's family built their home on Tibbetts Island, and Matthais learned about all that the island had to offer, returning to it throughout his life.

Gaeddert, Louann. *Breaking Free.* New York: Atheneum, 1994. Grades 5 and up.
  When Richard is sent to live on his uncle's farm, he resists the difficult life and resents the treatment of the slaves. He teaches a slave to read and helps her and her father escape to Canada. Eventually he is allowed to attend school.

———. *Hope.* New York: Atheneum, 1995. Grades 4 and up.
  Hope and her brother, John, are sent to live with Shakers after their mother dies. While Hope longs for the return of their father, John adjusts to the new life.

Hall, Donald. *The Milkman's Boy.* Illustrated by Greg Shed. New York: Walker, 1997. Grades 1 and up.
  The owner of the Graves Family Dairy resisted changing in the early 1900s. However, when his daughter got sick, he realized he had to pasteurize the milk.

———. *Old Home Day.* Illustrated by Emily Arnold McCully. San Diego, Calif.: Harcourt Brace, 1996. Grades 2 and up.
  The village of Blackwater Pond grew and developed during many generations. Then people left for larger cities. Finally the governor of New Hampshire proclaimed Old Home Day, revitalizing the New England town.

Hest, Amy. *When Jessie Came Across the Sea.* Illustrated by P. J. Lynch. Cambridge, Mass.: Candlewick Press, 1997. Grades 1 and up.

Leaving her homeland and grandmother was painful for Jessie, but she learned much in New York until she could send for her grandmother—just in time for her wedding.

Homes, Mary Z. *For Bread.* Austin, Tex.: Raintree Steck-Vaughn, 1992. Grades 4 and up.

Stefan, a young Polish boy, lives with his family in Buffalo, New York, in 1893. He struggles to find work to help his family in a time when many immigrants were out of work.

Hurwitz, Johanna. *Faraway Summer.* Illustrated by Mary Azarian. New York: Morrow, 1998. Grades 4 and up.

Dossi, who lives in the tenements of New York, is sent to a farm in Vermont as part of the Fresh Air Fund program in 1910. She discovers the challenges and joys of country life.

Jurmain, Suzanne. *Freedom's Sons: The True Story of the* Amistad *Mutiny.* New York: Lothrop, Lee & Shepard, 1998. Grades 5 and up.

When the *Amistad* and its crew of 53 African mutineers landed off the coast of America, one of the most compelling stories of freedom and justice began.

McMillan, Bruce. *Grandfather's Trolley.* Cambridge, Mass.: Candlewick Press, 1995. Grades Kindergarten and up.

Inspired by McMillan's grandfather who drove a trolley in Boston in the early 1900s, this beautifully photographed and illustrated book takes readers along for a charming ride.

Peck, Robert Newton. *Little Soup's Turkey.* Illustrated by Charles Robinson. New York: Dell, 1992. Grades 1 and up.

Rob and Soup create chaos in their Vermont hometown when they bring popcorn to their school play for Thanksgiving.

Pringle, Laurence. *One Room School.* Illustrated by Barbara Garrison. Honesdale, Pa.: Boyds Mills Press, 1998. Grades Kindergarten and up.

Pringle describes his first school experiences in a rural New York schoolhouse during the last year of World War II. The simple prints, framed as if photographs in a scrapbook, lend a warmth to the memoir.

Raschka, Chris. *Simple Gifts.* New York: Henry Holt, 1998. Grades 1 and up.

Inspired by Paul Klee, Raschka has created bold illustrations to enhance this traditional Shaker song.

Stone, Bruce. *Autumn of the Royal Tar.* New York: HarperCollins, 1995. Grades 5 and up.

When a ship burns off the coast of Maine, Nora yearns to help. Soon she is drawn into the tragedy as she helps to nurse a young boy who has been badly burned and who must also face the loss of his mother.

Turner, Ann. *Shaker Hearts.* Illustrated by Wendell Minor. New York: HarperCollins, 1997. Grades 1 and up.

The simple life and deep faith of this village is described through elegant poetry and simple illustrations.

Video

Let's Explore a Seashore. Washington, D.C.: National Geographic, 1994. 16 minutes. Grades 4
  and up.
  Search for clams along the rocky seashore of Maine.

New England. Washington, D.C.: National Geographic, 1983. 25 minutes. Grades 4 and up.
  Explore New Hampshire, Maine, Massachusetts, Vermont, Connecticut, and Rhode Island.

7
Mid-Atlantic States

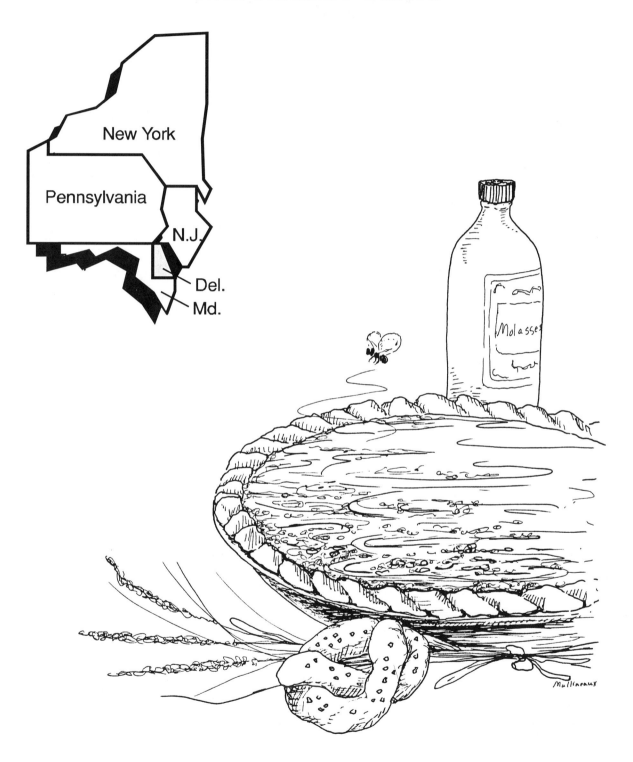

Mid-Atlantic States

Word List

- Apple butter
- Buckwheat
- Chestnuts
- Deer
- Elk
- Frankfurters
- Goose
- *Hutspot*
- Ice cream
- Jumbles
- *Kielbasa*
- *Lebkuchen*
- Molasses
- Nuts

- Oyster
- Puffards, Pulling the goose, Pepper pot
- Quakers
- *Rivel soup*
- Scrapple, Smearcase
- Tripe
- U.S. Senate Bean Soup
- Vinegar
- Washington Pie
- X
- Yeast
- Zwieback

JEWISH RYE BREAD

Ingredients

Starter

1 package dry yeast
2 cups very warm water
    (110 to 115 degrees)

½ teaspoon sugar
2 ¼ cups rye flour

Sponge

1 package dry yeast
¾ cup very warm water
1 cup white flour

Pinch of sugar
1 cup rye flour

Dough

1 tablespoon salt
4 tablespoons caraway seeds
2 ½ cups white flour

Yellow cornmeal
1 egg white
1 teaspoon water

Steps

Starter

1. Dissolve 1 package of yeast in 2 cups very warm water.
2. Stir in sugar and rye flour.
3. Cover and let stand at room temperature for 24 hours. Mixture will smell sour.

Sponge

1. Dissolve 1 package of yeast and the pinch of sugar in ¼ cup of the warm water.
2. Let stand until foamy.
3. In a large mixing bowl combine starter and all ingredients for sponge. Stir well.
4. Cover and let stand for 4 hours. Stir mixture.

Dough

1. To the sponge add salt, caraway seeds, and remaining white flour. Stir well.
2. Put dough onto a floured board. Knead for 10 minutes. Add extra flour if dough gets sticky.
3. Grease a large bowl. Roll dough around in it to grease dough.
4. Cover and let rise until dough has doubled in size (1 to 2 hours).
5. Sprinkle cornmeal on a large cookie sheet.
6. Form dough into 2 long loaves and put them on the cornmeal.
7. Let loaves rise until they have doubled in size (1 to 2 hours).
8. Preheat oven to 425 degrees.
9. Place a pan with 1 to 2 inches hot water on the bottom rack of the oven.
10. Mix egg white with 1 teaspoon water. Beat well.
11. Brush egg white mixture on top of loaves.
12. Bake loaves 20 minutes.
13. Turn oven down to 375 degrees and bake 15 minutes more or until the loaves make a hollow sound when tapped.
14. Cool loaves before slicing.
15. Wrap tightly after loaves have cooled.

Makes 2 loaves.

SOFT PRETZELS

Ingredients
1 package dry yeast
1 ½ teaspoons sugar
1 cup very warm water (110 to 115 degrees)
2 ½ cups flour
1 teaspoon salt
1 quart water
2 tablespoons baking soda
1 to 2 tablespoons coarse salt
Cornmeal
Mustard (optional)

Steps
1.   In a small bowl, dissolve yeast and sugar in ¼ cup of the warm water.
2.   In a large bowl, mix the flour and salt. Then stir in the remaining ¾ cup of the water.
3.   When yeast mixture is foamy, add it to the flour mixture and mix thoroughly.
4.   Put the mixture on a floured board and let it rest for 5 minutes.
5.   Wash and dry the large bowl. Grease it well.
6.   Knead dough 10 to 15 minutes, adding more flour if sticky.
7.   Put dough in greased bowl and cover tightly with plastic wrap.
8.   Let dough rise 1 hour or until doubled in size.
9.   Punch dough down.
10.   Cut dough into 8 pieces.
11.   Roll each piece into a thin tube 20 to 24 inches long.
12.   To shape the pretzel, grab each end of the tube and form a horseshoe shape with the curved part away from you.
13.   Twist the ends around each other and press firmly onto the loop of dough beneath them.
14.   Let pretzels rest on a floured board, under a towel, for 15 minutes.
15.   Preheat oven to 450 degrees.
16.   Simmer a quart of water in a medium pan. Add baking soda.
17.   Carefully place a few pretzels at a time in water for 30 seconds on each side.
18.   Remove pretzels from water. Pat dry with a towel.
19.   Lightly dust a baking sheet with cornmeal.
20.   Place pretzels on baking sheet and sprinkle with coarse salt.
21.   Bake 10 to 12 minutes or until light brown.
22.   Serve warm with mustard squeezed on top.

Makes 8.

MATZO BALL SOUP

Ingredients
1 quart chicken stock
4 eggs
¼ cup oil
½ teaspoon baking powder
1 ½ cups matzo meal
1 teaspoon chopped parsley
¼ teaspoon salt

Steps
1. Pour chicken stock into a large saucepan and boil.
2. Beat eggs in a large mixing bowl.
3. Add oil to eggs. Beat well.
4. Slowly stir in baking powder, matzoh meal, parsley, and salt.
5. Wet hands and shape mixture into small balls.
6. Drop balls into simmering chicken stock.
7. Cook about 20 minutes until balls are firm and cooked through.

Serves 5 to 6.

MARYLAND FRIED OYSTERS

Ingredients
2 dozen shucked oysters
2 eggs
2 tablespoons milk
1 teaspoon salt
¼ teaspoon pepper
1 cup dried bread crumbs
Margarine for frying
Tartar sauce

Steps
1. Wash oysters and pat dry.
2. Beat eggs in a small bowl.
3. Add milk, salt, and pepper. Mix well.
4. Dip oysters in egg mixture. Dip in bread crumbs.
5. Melt margarine in a large frying pan over medium heat.
6. Cook breaded oysters in margarine until browned on both sides.
7. Serve with tartar sauce.

Makes 24 oysters.

MARYLAND CRAB CAKES

Ingredients

3 tablespoons butter or margarine
3 tablespoons chopped onions
1 ⅔ cups soft bread crumbs
1 ½ pounds crab meat
2 eggs

½ teaspoon dry mustard
Salt, pepper, and paprika (to taste)
½ cup flour
Butter for frying

Steps

1. Melt butter in a large saucepan over medium heat.
2. Cook onion in butter until it is soft and clear.
3. Remove from heat.
4. Stir in bread crumbs, crab meat, eggs, mustard, salt, pepper, and paprika.
5. If the mixture is too dry, add a little milk.
6. Shape mixture into flat cakes.
7. Roll cakes in flour.
8. Melt butter in a frying pan over medium heat.
9. Fry both sides of crabcake until brown and cooked through.

Serves 6.

HOT POTATO SALAD

Ingredients

6 potatoes
1 stalk celery, chopped
3 hard-boiled eggs, diced
1 onion, finely chopped
1 tablespoon parsley, chopped
4 slices bacon, chopped

2 eggs, well beaten
1 cup sugar
½ teaspoon salt
½ teaspoon pepper
½ cup vinegar, mixed with ¼ cup water
1 tablespoon mustard

Steps

1. Put whole potatoes (in skins) in a large saucepan and cover with water.
2. Boil potatoes for 20 minutes.
3. Remove from heat and peel potatoes.
4. Dice potatoes and put into a large bowl.
5. Add celery, hard-boiled eggs, onion, and parsley to potatoes. Stir lightly.
6. Fry bacon over medium-high heat until crisp. Remove skillet from heat.
7. Remove bacon from skillet with slotted spoon and drain on paper towels. (Keep bacon fat in skillet.)
8. Put eggs in a medium bowl. Add the sugar, salt, pepper, vinegar, mustard and water. Stir well.
9. Put skillet with bacon fat back on the stove over medium heat.
10. Pour egg mixture into bacon fat. Stir until mixture thickens, about 10 minutes.
11. Put mixture over potatoes and mix lightly. Stir in crispy bacon.
12. Serve warm.

Serves 6 to 8.

SOUTH PHILLY CHEESE STEAK SANDWICHES

Ingredients

4 tablespoons margarine
2 large onions
12 frozen sandwich steaks
   (the thin, leathery sandwich steaks)

6 Italian rolls, sliced lengthwise
6 slices American cheese
Salt or ketchup

Steps

1. Heat a large griddle over medium heat.
2. Melt margarine on griddle.
3. Slice onions and cook on griddle.
4. As the onion slices turn soft and brown, push them over to the edges of the griddle.
5. Put thawed sandwich steaks on the griddle and brown on both sides.
6. Put 1 slice of cheese on every other piece of steak. Melt cheese.
7. Put one cheese-covered steak on top of another steak. Add onions. Place in a roll.
8. Add salt and ketchup, if desired.

Makes 6.

SNICKERDOODLES

Ingredients

$\frac{1}{2}$ cup butter, softened
$\frac{3}{4}$ cup sugar
1 egg
2 cups flour
1 $\frac{1}{4}$ teaspoon baking powder

$\frac{1}{2}$ teaspoon salt
$\frac{1}{2}$ cup milk
1 teaspoon vanilla
$\frac{1}{4}$ cup sugar
1 tablespoon cinnamon

Steps

1. Preheat oven to 325 degrees.
2. Stir butter with a wooden spoon until creamy.
3. Add sugar. Mix well.
4. Add egg. Mix well.
5. Mix flour, baking powder, and salt in a separate bowl.
6. Add $\frac{1}{3}$ of the flour mixture to butter mixture. Stir well.
7. Add $\frac{1}{2}$ of the milk to the butter mixture. Stir well.
8. Add $\frac{1}{3}$ of the flour mixture and $\frac{1}{2}$ of the milk. Stir well.
9. Stir in the vanilla.
10. Add the remaining flour mixture. Stir well.
11. Drop heaping teaspoonfuls of dough about 2 inches apart onto a greased cookie sheet.
12. Mix $\frac{1}{4}$ cup sugar and 1 tablespoon cinnamon in a small bowl.
13. Sprinkle sugar and cinnamon mixture over the mounds of dough.
14. Bake 10 to 15 minutes or until cookies are lightly browned around the edges.
15. Cool. Store in a tightly covered container.

Makes 3 to 4 dozen cookies.

PENNSYLVANIA DUTCH SHOO-FLY PIE

Ingredients
1 9-inch unbaked pie shell

Molasses mixture
½ teaspoon baking soda
¾ cup hot water
¾ cup molasses

Crumb mixture
1 ½ cups flour
¾ cup brown sugar
½ teaspoon cinnamon
¼ teaspoon nutmeg
¼ teaspoon ginger
¼ cup butter

Steps
1. Stir baking soda into hot water until it dissolves.
2. Add molasses. Stir well.
3. Pour ⅓ of this mixture into the pie shell.
4. Mix the flour, brown sugar, cinnamon, nutmeg, and ginger well.
5. Cut in the butter until mixture is crumbly.
6. Sprinkle ⅓ of the crumb mixture over the molasses mixture in the pie shell.
7. Repeat with half of the remaining molasses mixture and half of the remaining crumb mixture.
8. Use the remaining portions of each mixture to make a third set of layers.
9. Bake pie at 425 degrees for 10 minutes.
10. Reduce heat to 350 degrees. Bake for 30 minutes.

Serves 8.

NEW YORK CHEESECAKE

Ingredients

Crust
1 cup flour
⅓ cup sugar
½ teaspoon vanilla
8 tablespoons softened butter
1 egg yolk

Filling
24 ounces cream cheese, softened
1 cup sugar
4 eggs
3 tablespoons sour cream
1 teaspoon grated lemon rind
2 tablespoons flour
½ teaspoon vanilla

Steps

Crust
1. Combine flour, sugar, and vanilla in a large mixing bowl.
2. Mix in butter and egg yolk until mixture forms a soft dough. Add a small amount of cold water if dough is too dry. Do not over mix.
3. Chill dough 1 hour in refrigerator.
4. Preheat oven to 400 degrees.
5. Grease the bottom and sides of a 9-inch springform pan.
6. Roll dough out on a floured board.
7. Using the bottom of the pan as a guide, cut a circle out of the dough.
8. Press the circle of dough onto the bottom of the pan.
9. Press the rest of the dough evenly onto the sides the pan.
10. Bake the dough 15 minutes. Remove from oven.
11. Reduce the oven temperature to 275 degrees.

Filling
1. Beat cream cheese with an electric mixer until smooth.
2. Beat in sugar, eggs, sour cream, lemon rind, flour, and vanilla. Pour cream cheese mixture into cooled crust.
3. Bake at 275 degrees one hour.
4. Turn off oven and let cheesecake sit in oven for 15 more minutes.
5. Remove from oven. Cool completely before serving.

Note: To soften cream cheese, let stand at room temperature 1 to 2 hours.

Serves 8 to 10.

From *Cooking Up U.S. History*, Second Edition. © 1999 Suzanne I. Barchers and Patricia C. Marden. Teacher Ideas Press. (800) 237-6124.

FUNNEL CAKES

Ingredients

1 ½ cups flour
½ teaspoon salt
¾ teaspoon baking soda
½ teaspoon cream of tartar
2 ½ tablespoons sugar
1 egg
1 ¼ cups milk
Oil for deep-fat frying
Large, tin funnel
Powdered sugar for sprinkling on top

Steps

1. Put flour, salt, baking soda, cream of tartar, and sugar into a large bowl. Mix well.
2. Beat egg in a small bowl. Stir in milk.
3. Add egg mixture to flour mixture. Beat until smooth.
4. Pour 1 to 1 ½ inches oil into a large skillet and heat to 375 degrees.
5. Put your finger over the small end of the funnel. Pour some of the batter into the funnel.
6. Remove your finger from the funnel and pour the batter into the hot oil in a circular motion.
7. Fry until lightly browned and turn over carefully with a fork or slotted spoon.
8. Fry on the other side until brown. Remove from oil onto paper towels.
9. Repeat, pouring small amounts of batter into hot fat and frying until all batter has been used up.
10. Sprinkle funnel cakes with powdered sugar and serve.

Serves 4.

MINEHAHA CAKE

Ingredients

Cake
½ cup butter, softened
2 cups sugar
2 ½ teaspoons baking powder
¾ cup milk
1 ⅔ cups flour
5 egg whites at room temperature

Icing
2 cups sugar
3 tablespoons water
2 egg whites at room temperature
Dash salt
¾ cup raisins
¾ cup walnuts
1 teaspoon vanilla

Steps

Cake
1. Preheat oven to 350 degrees.
2. Cream butter with a wooden spoon.
3. Stir in sugar and baking powder.
4. Divide milk and flour into 3 equal parts. Begin with the flour and alternately beat in each part.
5. Put eggs in a medium-sized glass or metal bowl.
6. Add a dash of salt.
7. Whip with an electric mixer on high until soft peaks form.
8. Gently fold flour mixture into the egg whites until well mixed.
9. Grease 2 9-inch round cake pans.
10. Pour cake batter into the pans.
11. Bake about 25 minutes or until done in the center.
12. Let cool.

Icing
1. Put sugar and water in a heavy medium-sized saucepan.
2. Boil over medium-high heat until the mixture drops from a spoon, forming a hair.
3. Put egg whites in a small bowl with high sides.
4. Add salt.
5. Whip until the egg whites are thick and foamy.
6. Pour sugar over the egg whites and beat until thick.
7. Add raisins, walnuts, and vanilla. Stir well.
8. Spread icing on cooled cake between the layers and on the top.

Serves 10 to 12.

From *Cooking Up U.S. History*, Second Edition. © 1999 Suzanne I. Barchers and Patricia C. Marden. Teacher Ideas Press. (800) 237-6124.

PENNSYLVANIA DUTCH APPLE MERINGUE

Ingredients

3 to 4 large apples
Water
⅓ cup sugar
2 tablespoons butter
½ teaspoon nutmeg

½ teaspoon cinnamon
1 tablespoon lemon juice
3 eggs
⅓ cup powdered sugar
1 teaspoon vanilla

Steps

1. Preheat oven to 400 degrees.
2. Peel, slice, and core apples.
3. Place apples in a medium saucepan with about 1 inch of water.
4. Cook over medium heat until apples are soft.
5. Put 2 heaping cups of apples in a large mixing bowl.
6. Stir in sugar, butter, nutmeg, cinnamon, and lemon juice.
7. Separate egg yolks from egg whites.
8. Beat egg yolks.
9. Add the apple mixture. Beat well.
10. Grease a 9-inch square baking pan.
11. Pour apple mixture into greased pan.
12. Bake in oven for 15 minutes.
13. While mixture is baking, put egg whites into a medium-sized glass or metal bowl.
14. Beat egg whites with an electric mixer on high until stiff.
15. Slowly add powdered sugar and vanilla. Continue to beat until completely mixed in. This is meringue.
16. Remove apple mixture from oven after 15 minutes.
17. Pour meringue over the top of the apple mixture.
18. Reduce the oven temperature to 325 degrees.
19. Return the pan to the oven.
20. Bake until the meringue is slightly browned.
21. Cool and cut into rectangles.

Makes 12 bars.

DELAWARE SNOW CREAM

Ingredients

1 egg
1 can evaporated milk, chilled
2 teaspoons vanilla

¾ cup sugar
Snow

Steps

1. Beat egg in a large mixing bowl.
2. Beat in the milk, vanilla, and sugar.
3. Find some fresh, clean snow.
4. Carefully fold snow into the egg mixture until the snow cream is the desired texture.

Serves 3 to 6.

From *Cooking Up U.S. History*, Second Edition. © 1999 Suzanne I. Barchers and Patricia C. Marden. Teacher Ideas Press. (800) 237-6124.

Library Links

Library Link 1:   Rye is grown in Pennsylvania. What other grains are grown in Pennsylvania?

Library Link 2:   When were the first commercial pretzel bakeries established?

Library Link 3:   On what occasion are matzo balls often eaten by the Jewish people?

Library Link 4:   Study a map of Maryland. Why were oysters so plentiful in that area?

Library Link 5:   What are soft-shell crabs?

Library Link 6:   For many years, Jersey and Guernsey cows gave the milk and the cream used for cheese production. What kind of cows are used now? Why?

Library Link 7:   Where did the name *Snickerdoodle* come from?

Library Link 8:   How did shoo-fly pie get its name?

Library Link 9:   Cheesecake came from the Germans, who often used zwieback for the crust. What is zwieback?

Library Link 10:   What Dutch man explored Delaware in 1609?

Library Link 11:   Why do many Pennsylvania Dutch have hex signs on their barns?

Library Link 12:   What U.S. first lady made ice cream the official White House dessert?

From *Cooking Up U.S. History*, Second Edition. © 1999 Suzanne I. Barchers and Patricia C. Marden. Teacher Ideas Press. (800) 237-6124.

Bibliography—Mid-Atlantic States

Nonfiction

Fisher, Leonard Everett. *Ellis Island: Gateway to the New World.* New York: Holiday House, 1986. Grades 4 and up.
First purchased from the Native American Indians in 1634, Ellis Island was a fort before it became an immigration station. Fisher uses actual accounts and photographs and drawings to tell the story of the immigrants who came through Ellis Island.

Graymont, Barbara. *Indians of North America: The Iroquois.* New York: Chelsea House, 1988. Grades 4 and up.
In upstate New York, the Iroquois lived and fought alongside many other tribes. Their history and struggle for survival are described with black-and-white and color photographs.

St. George, Judith. *Mason and Dixon's Line of Fire.* New York: G. P. Putnam's Sons, 1991. Grades 5 and up.
The 200-year history of the problems associated with the boundary between Pennsylvania and Maryland is detailed along with maps, drawings, and art.

Fiction

Ammon, Richard. *An Amish Christmas.* Illustrated by Pamela Patrick. New York: Atheneum, 1996. All ages.
Recounts the story of a family as they prepare for and enjoy Christmas, and incorporates information about the Amish culture.

Lasky, Kathryn. *Dreams in the Golden Country: The Diary of Zipporah Feldman, a Jewish Immigrant Girl.* New York: Scholastic, 1998. Grades 4 and up.
The diary format lends interest to the story of Zippy's life as a new immigrant in New York City in the early 1900s.

McCully, Emily Arnold. *The Ballot Box Battle.* New York: Alfred A. Knopf, 1996. Grades 2 and up.
Cordelia lives next door to Elizabeth Cady Stanton. While taking riding lessons from Stanton, Cordelia learns how she came to fight for equality.

Rappaport, Doreen. *Trouble at the Mines.* Illustrated by Joan Sandin. New York: Thomas Y. Crowell, 1987. Grades 2 and up.
This is based on the true story of the 1898 miners' strike in Arnst, Pennsylvania, and is about Rosie, who marched with Mother Jones, the miners' angel.

Robinet, Harriette Gillem. *Washington City Is Burning.* New York: Simon & Schuster, 1996. Grades 4 and up.
Virginia has come to work at the White House in 1814, just when the British burn much of the city. Her work also includes helping slaves escape to freedom, and her bravery is demonstrated in this rich story.

Yolen, Jane. *The Gift of Sarah Barker*. New York: Viking, 1981. Grades 6 and up.
   In a fictional town similar to a Shaker community, two teenagers fall in love, risking expulsion from their homes.

Videos

The East. Washington, D.C.: National Geographic, 1989. 20 minutes. Grades 4 and up.
   Travel through the Atlantic coastal plain, the Piedmont, and the Appalachian highlands.

The Mid-Atlantic States. Washington, D.C.: National Geographic, 1983. 27 minutes. Grades 4 and up.
   Explore New York, New Jersey, Pennsylvania, Delaware, Maryland, and Washington, D.C.

The Quest for Freedom: The Harriet Tubman Story. Richardson, Tex.: Grace Products Corporation, 1992. 40 minutes. Grades 4 and up.
   This video emphasizes Harriet Tubman's life in Maryland and her efforts to lead people north. The focus occurs before the Civil War. Includes a teacher's guide.

1600 Pennsylvania Avenue: The White House. Washington, D.C.: National Geographic, 1997. 84 minutes. Grades 4 and up.
   Tour the White House with these two videos. Teacher's guide.

Washington, D.C. Washington, D.C.: National Geographic, 1983. 20 minutes. Grades 6 and up.
   Tour the nation's capital.

8
The Southeast

The Southeast

Word List

- Ashcake
- Burgoo, Bouillabaisse
- Corn pone, Chitterlings
- Duck
- Eggnog, Egg bread
- Fried pie, Filé powder
- Grits, Goobers, Gumbo
- Hush Puppies, Hoecakes, Hog jowls
- Indigo
- Jambalaya
- Kumquats
- Lye-hominy, Lima beans
- Mullet
- Nutmeg
- Okra
- Periwinkle clams, Persimmon, Peccary
- Quince honey
- Redfish
- Scrapple, Scuppernong
- Tobbaco, Tangerine, Tutti Frutti
- Upside-down cake
- Vegetable
- Watermelon
- X
- Yams
- Zucchini pudding

GRITS

Ingredients
2 cups unprocessed grits
4 cups water
¾ teaspoon salt

Steps
1. Wash grits well.
2. Soak grits in water overnight.
3. Pour water off grits.
4. Put grits in a large saucepan. Add fresh water to cover.
5. Bring to a boil.
6. Add salt and cook over low heat for about 2 hours or until thickened.
7. Serve while hot.

Makes 6 cups.

FRIED GRITS

Ingredients
2 ½ cups cooked grits
2 eggs
1 cup seasoned bread crumbs
Butter or margarine for frying
Optional: Maple syrup

Steps
1. Pour hot, cooked grits into a loaf pan to cool.
2. Cut into slices.
3. Beat eggs in a bowl.
4. Dip slice of grits into eggs. Coat both sides.
5. Dip slice into bread crumbs. Cover both sides.
6. Heat butter in a large frying pan over medium-high heat.
7. Place slices of breaded grits into frying pan and fry on both sides until browned.
8. Add maple syrup, if desired.
9. Eat while warm.

Serves 6.

HUSH PUPPIES

Ingredients

1 ¼ cups white cornmeal
1 teaspoon baking powder
1 teaspoon salt
⅛ teaspoon pepper
¾ teaspoon sugar
⅓ cup milk
¼ cup water
1 egg, beaten
Oil for frying

Steps

1. In a large bowl combine cornmeal, baking powder, salt, pepper, and sugar.
2. In a small bowl mix the milk, water, and beaten egg.
3. Pour milk mixture into cornmeal mixture and stir well.
4. Put oil in a frying pan ¼ inch deep.
5. Heat oil to 375 degrees.
6. Drop tablespoonfuls of dough into the hot oil.
7. Fry until browned on all sides.
8. Drain hush puppies on paper towels.
9. Serve warm.

Makes 16 to 20.

SOUTHERN PEANUT SOUP

Ingredients

5 tablespoons butter
½ large onion, chopped
1 large stalk celery, chopped
2 tablespoons flour
1 cup natural peanut butter (no additives)
5 cups chicken broth
1 teaspoon Worcestershire sauce
1 teaspoon salt
½ cup chopped peanuts

Steps

1. Put butter in a skillet over medium heat.
2. Add onion and celery. Cook until tender.
3. Stir in flour.
4. Stir in peanut butter.
5. Add the broth and seasonings. Stir well.
6. Pour into bowls. Sprinkle with chopped peanuts.

Serves 4.

SHORT'NIN' BREAD

Ingredients
1 ¼ cups butter, softened
½ cup brown sugar
¼ cup confectioner's sugar
½ teaspoon salt
½ teaspoon cinnamon
2 ½ cups flour

Steps
1. Cream butter.
2. Stir in both sugars and beat until creamy.
3. Add salt and cinnamon and stir well.
4. Add flour and mix well with back of a wooden spoon. If mixture becomes too stiff to stir, work it with your hands.
5. Place dough on an ungreased cookie sheet.
6. Press into a rectangle about ½ inch thick.
7. Prick dough all over with a fork.
8. Cut lines into dough to make squares.
9. Bake at 350 degrees about 15 to 20 minutes until slightly brown at the edges.
10. While still warm, cut into squares on lines you cut into the dough.
11. Remove from pan.

Makes 3 to 4 dozen.

From *Cooking Up U.S. History*, Second Edition. © 1999 Suzanne I. Barchers and Patricia C. Marden. Teacher Ideas Press. (800) 237-6124.

SEAFOOD GUMBO

Ingredients
1 ¼ cups oil
1 ¼ cups flour
1 ½ cups chopped onion
½ cup chopped celery
¼ cup chopped green pepper
2 cloves of garlic, chopped
2 tomatoes, peeled and chopped
3 quarts chicken broth
¼ cup chopped parsley
½ teaspoon pepper
1 teaspoon salt
3 bay leaves
2 pounds small shrimp, shelled
½ pound crabmeat
2 dozen oysters and their juice
3 cups cooked rice

Steps
1. Heat 1 cup of the oil in saucepan over medium heat.
2. Add flour and stir.
3. Stir and cook over low heat for about 30 minutes until mixture, called roux, is dark brown.
4. Pour ¼ cup oil into a large soup pot.
5. Heat over medium heat. Add onion and cook until clear.
6. Add celery, green pepper, and garlic to onion. Cook 5 minutes.
7. Add roux to onion mixture and cook 10 more minutes, stirring constantly.
8. Add tomatoes to mixture.
9. Add chicken broth and turn heat to medium high.
10. Stir well and add parsley, pepper, salt, and bay leaves.
11. Bring to a boil.
12. Lower heat and simmer for 45 minutes.
13. Add shrimp and crabmeat and bring to a boil.
14. Remove from heat.
15. Chop oysters into large pieces.
16. Add oysters and their juice to mixture and stir well.
17. Remove bay leaves.
18. Put some rice in the bottom of each serving bowl and pour gumbo over it.
19. Eat while hot.

Serves 10.

MASSIE STACK CAKE

Ingredients
¾ cup shortening, softened
¾ cup sugar
⅓ cup brown sugar
1 cup molasses
3 eggs
4 cups flour
½ teaspoon baking soda
¾ teaspoon salt
1 teaspoon ginger
1 cup milk
3 cups applesauce
½ teaspoon cinnamon

Steps
1. Cream shortening in a large mixing bowl.
2. Stir in sugars and molasses. Beat well.
3. Add eggs. Beat well.
4. Mix flour, baking soda, salt, and ginger in a medium bowl.
5. Add about ⅓ of this mixture to shortening mixture and stir well.
6. Add ½ of the milk and stir.
7. Add ½ of the remaining flour mixture and stir.
8. Add the remaining milk and stir.
9. Add remaining flour mixture and stir well.
10. Grease 6 9-inch round cake pans.
11. Pour equal amounts of the batter into the 6 cake pans.
12. Bake at 375 degrees for 15 to 20 minutes or until a toothpick put into the middle comes out clean.
13. Remove cake layers from pans.
14. Let layers cool.
15. Stack cooled cake layers, putting equal amounts (about ½ cup) of applesauce in between each layer.
16. Sprinkle cinnamon on top layer of applesauce and cake.

Serves 10 to 12.

CHICKEN, GRAVY, AND DUMPLINGS

Ingredients

Chicken

3 ½ to 4 pounds chicken
¼ cup flour
¼ teaspoon salt
¼ cup shortening
1 small onion, chopped
1 clove garlic, chopped
1 stick celery, chopped

2 cups water
1 bay leaf
2 chicken bouillon cubes or packages
3 tablespoons flour
2 tablespoons water
Salt and pepper (to taste)

Dumplings

1 ½ cups flour
2 teaspoons baking powder
½ teaspoon salt
¼ teaspoon pepper

1 tablespoon dried parsley
½ cup shortening, softened
6 tablespoons cold water

Steps

Chicken
1. Cut chicken into serving-sized pieces.
2. Put ¼ cup flour and ¼ teaspoon salt in a plastic bag.
3. Add the chicken pieces and shake well, coating the chicken with the flour mixture.
4. In large heavy skillet, heat ¼ cup shortening over medium heat.
5. Add chicken to hot oil and cook until browned on both sides.
6. Remove chicken.
7. Add chopped onion, garlic, and celery to skillet. Cook until soft.
8. Return chicken to skillet.
9. Add water, bay leaf, and bouillon. Mix.
10. Heat until it simmers.
11. Mix 3 tablespoons flour with 2 tablespoons water.
12. Stir flour mixture into simmering chicken and broth.
13. Cover and simmer for 30 minutes or until chicken is well done.

Dumplings
1. Combine flour, baking powder, salt, pepper, and parsley.
2. Cut in shortening until mixture forms balls.
3. Stir in cold water.
4. Remove cover from chicken. Drop in dumpling dough by the tablespoon on top of chicken.
5. Cover and cook 15 to 20 minutes or until dumplings are dry and cooked through.
6. Serve chicken and dumplings together with gravy over both.

Serves 6.

From *Cooking Up U.S. History*, Second Edition. © 1999 Suzanne I. Barchers and Patricia C. Marden. Teacher Ideas Press. (800) 237-6124.

SWEET POTATO PIE

Ingredients
2 to 3 large sweet potatoes
½ cup butter
1 cup sugar
2 eggs
½ cup evaporated milk
1 teaspoon vanilla
¼ teaspoon salt
½ teaspoon cinnamon
½ teaspoon nutmeg
¼ teaspoon allspice
1 9-inch unbaked pie crust

Steps
1. Bake or boil sweet potatoes until soft. Peel.
2. Mash potatoes and measure. Use only 2 to 2 ½ cups mashed potatoes.
3. Cream butter and sugar together. Beat until light.
4. Add eggs. Mix well.
5. Stir in potatoes, milk, vanilla, salt, cinnamon, nutmeg, and allspice.
6. Pour mixture into pie crust.
7. Bake about 40 minutes at 375 degrees or until knife inserted in center comes out clean.

Serves 8.

PEANUT CAKE

Ingredients

Cake

1 ¼ cups peanut butter
½ cup margarine, softened
2 cups brown sugar
5 eggs
2 cups flour
2 teaspoons baking powder
½ teaspoon salt
¾ cup milk
2 teaspoons vanilla

Frosting

½ cup peanut butter
¼ cup margarine, softened
4 cups confectioner's sugar
½ cup milk
2 teaspoons vanilla

Steps

Cake

1. Cream peanut butter and margarine together in a large mixing bowl.
2. Add sugar and beat well.
3. Add eggs, one at a time, beating well after each one.
4. Mix flour, baking powder, and salt together in a small bowl.
5. Add ⅓ of the flour mixture to butters and sugar and mix well.
6. Add about ½ of the milk. Mix well.
7. Add ½ of the remaining flour mixture. Mix well.
8. Add the remaining milk. Mix well.
9. Add the remaining flour mixture. Mix well.
10. Add vanilla. Mix well.
11. Grease a 9-by-13-inch pan.
12. Pour batter into pan.
13. Bake at 350 degree for 45 minutes or until a toothpick inserted in the center comes out clean.
14. Cool cake in pan.
15. Make frosting and frost cake.

Frosting

1. Cream peanut butter and margarine together.
2. Stir in half of the confectioner's sugar. Mix well.
3. Add the rest of the sugar.
4. Add enough milk to make a smooth frosting.
5. Stir in vanilla.
6. Beat until smooth.

Serves 12 to 15.

CONFEDERATE SOLDIER CAKES

Ingredients

6 eggs
1 ½ cups sugar
1 ¼ cups candied fruit

½ cup blanched almonds
2 cups flour

Steps

1. Separate egg yolks from egg whites.
2. Beat egg yolks with an electric mixer until they are thick and lemon colored.
3. Gradually add sugar and beat well.
4. Put ½ cup flour in a small bowl and stir in candied fruit.
5. Stir fruit into egg yolk mixture.
6. In a large bowl, combine egg whites and the rest of the flour.
7. Beat until thick.
8. Stir yolk mixture in. Mix well.
9. Fold in almonds.
10. Grease a 15-by-10-by-1-inch pan.
11. Pour batter into the pan.
12. Bake at 425 degrees for 10 minutes.
13. Remove from oven and cut into bars.
14. Put bars back in oven for 5 more minutes.
15. Remove from oven and cool.

Makes 24 to 32.

KEY LIME PIE

Ingredients

1 can sweetened condensed milk
2 tablespoons lemon juice
6 tablespoons key lime juice
1 tablespoon grated lime peel
3 eggs separated
¼ teaspoon cream of tartar
1 baked pastry shell
Whipped cream for topping

Steps

1. Pour sweetened condensed milk into a large bowl.
2. Add juices and lime peel. Stir well.
3. Beat egg yolks. Stir into juice mixture.
4. Beat egg whites with cream of tartar in a small bowl until stiff and glossy.
5. Gently fold egg whites into juice mixture.
6. Pour into pie shell. Chill.
7. Serve topped with whipped cream.

Serves 6 to 8.

From *Cooking Up U.S. History*, Second Edition. © 1999 Suzanne I. Barchers and Patricia C. Marden. Teacher Ideas Press. (800) 237-6124.

CREOLE PECAN PRALINES

Ingredients
2 cups brown sugar
1 cup boiling water
¼ cup molasses
4 cups pecan halves
Buttered wax paper, or plastic slab

Steps
1. Put sugar into saucepan.
2. Add water. Stir well.
3. Put saucepan over low heat.
4. Add molasses. Stir until syrup forms soft ball when dropped into cold water.
5. Remove from heat. Stir in nuts.
6. Drop about 2 tablespoons of syrup mixture at a time onto buttered wax paper.
7. Let cool.
8. Store in tins.

Serves 8 to 10.

PECAN PIE

Ingredients
3 eggs
½ cup sugar
¼ teaspoon salt
1 cup dark corn syrup
1 teaspoon vanilla
1 ½ cups pecans
1 pie shell, unbaked
Whipped cream, if desired

Steps
1. Preheat oven to 450 degrees.
2. Beat eggs in a large bowl.
3. Add sugar, salt, corn syrup, and vanilla. Stir well.
4. Pour pecans into pie shell.
5. Pour egg mixture over pecans.
6. Bake in oven for 10 minutes.
7. Reduce heat to 350 degrees.
8. Bake for 35 minutes longer.
9. Remove from oven.
10. Add whipped cream if desired. Eat warm or cold.

Serves 8.

From *Cooking Up U.S. History*, Second Edition. © 1999 Suzanne I. Barchers and Patricia C. Marden. Teacher Ideas Press. (800) 237-6124.

Library Links

Library Link 1: What was usually served with grits for breakfast?

Library Link 2: What is the source of grits?

Library Link 3: What is a popular theory for how hush puppies got their name?

Library Link 4: What childhood song is about short'nin' bread?

Library Link 5: What state is most famous for its gumbo?

Library Link 6: What special event were stack cakes used for in the South?

Library Link 7: What kind of dumplings were called blue marbles?

Library Link 8: What famous king loved sweet potato pie so much he imported sweet potatoes from Spain?

Library Link 9: How many tons of peanut butter do Americans eat each year?

Library Link 10: Find out how to make candied fruit.

Bibliography—The Southeast

Nonfiction

Bial, Raymond. *Where Lincoln Walked.* New York: Walker, 1997. Grades 3 and up.
  Focusing on Lincoln's early years, the rich photographs enhance a fascinating overview of Lincoln's homes, schooling, and family life.

Micucci, Charles. *The Life and Times of the Peanut.* Boston: Houghton Mifflin, 1997. Grades 2 and up.
  This lively, colorful text covers the history, cultivation, and many uses of peanuts.

Parks, Rosa, and Jim Haskins. *I Am Rosa Parks.* Illustrated by Wil Clay. New York: Dial, 1997. Grades 1 and up.
  This easy-to-read chapter book describes Rosa Parks's experiences that led to her work for fair treatment for black people.

Fiction

Beatty, Patricia. *Be Ever Hopeful, Hannalee.* New York: Morrow Junior Books, 1988. Grades 5 and up.
  The Civil War is finally over and instead of returning home to stay, Hannalee must join her brother in Atlanta, where she faces hard work and danger.

Creech, Sharon. *Chasing Redbird.* New York: HarperCollins, 1997. Grades 5 and up.
  Zinny, who lives with her family in Kentucky, yearns for a place of her own. When she discovers a trail beginning at their farm, she begins to clear it, discovering a place of her own and truths about herself.

Crofford, Emily. *A Place to Belong.* Minneapolis, Minn.: Carolrhoda Books, 1994. Grades 5 and up.
  The McLinn family has lost their farm in Tennessee during the Depression and is moving to Arkansas. Their work on a plantation leaves little time for Talmadge to pursue the schooling he longs for.

George, Jean Craighead. *Everglades.* Illustrated by Wendell Minor. New York: HarperCollins, 1995. Grades 2 and up.
  Through the voice of a storyteller, children learn about the ecosystem of the Everglades and the threats to it that exist.

Grover, Wayne. *Dolphin Treasure.* Illustrated by Jim Fowler. New York: Greenwillow Books, 1996. Grades 2 and up.
  In this easy chapter book, a scuba diver describes a tale of treasure hunting, being lost in a storm, and being rescued by a family of dolphins off the coast of Florida.

Hooks, William H. *Freedom's Fruit*. Illustrated by James Ransome. New York: Alfred A. Knopf, 1996. Grades 2 and up.

Mama Marina, a conjure woman, desperately wants to free her daughter from slavery. At the request of her master, she casts a spell on the vineyard, but then turns the spell to her advantage to save her daughter and her daughter's beloved.

Hopkinson, Deborah. *Sweet Clara and the Freedom Quilt*. Illustrated by James Ransome. New York: Alfred A. Knopf, 1993. Grades 3 and up.

Clara lives in the big house on a plantation, but she longs to be with her mother. When she hears about the Underground Railroad, she uses her quilting skills to create a map imbedded in the quilt.

Lyons, Mary E. *Letters from a Slave Girl: The Story of Harriet Jacobs*. New York: Charles Scribner's Sons, 1992. Grades 5 and up.

Based on Harriet Jacobs's life, her struggles to survive slavery and escape to the North are chronicled in a series of compelling letters.

Paulsen, Gary. *Nightjohn*. New York: Dell, 1993. Grades 4 and up.

In this brief but intense story, Nightjohn returns from freedom to teach reading to other slaves. Contains some violence.

Pinkney, Gloria Jean. *Back Home*. Illustrated by Jerry Pinkney. New York: Dial, 1992. Grades 1 and up.

When Ernestine takes the train from up north to visit her family in North Carolina, she finds herself hoping her cousin Jack will be her friend. After a slow start, she discovers that both Jack and the farm will be missed when she returns to the city.

Sherman, Charlotte Watson. *Eli and the Swamp Man*. Illustrated by James Ransome. New York: HarperCollins, 1996. Grades 2 and up.

Eli would rather set out alone to find his father in Alaska than go to Mardi Gras in New Orleans with his stepfather and family. On the way, his encounter with the dreaded Swamp Man helps him resolve his feelings.

Siegelson, Kim. *The Terrible, Wonderful Tellin' at Hog Hammock*. Illustrated by Eric Velasquez. New York: HarperCollins, 1996. Grades 4 and up.

Traditional storytelling is an important part of the culture on Sapelo Island off the coast of Georgia. Jonas, grieving over the death of his grandfather, tries to carry on grandfather's tradition of being an outstanding teller.

Staples, Suzanne Fisher. *Dangerous Skies*. New York: HarperTrophy, 1996. Grades 5 and up.

Buck and Tunes' friendship is severely tested when they find a body along the Virginia shoreline, and Tunes tries to distance herself from the discovery. Though Buck is certain he knows the truth, Tunes faces accusations of being the killer. Although a compelling story, it should be preread because of the themes of murder and molestation.

White, Ruth. *Belle Prater's Boy.* New York: Farrar, Straus & Giroux, 1996. Grades 4 and up.
Woodrow and his cousin Gypsy become close when Woodrow comes to live with his grandparents in Virginia. Each has lost a parent, and they learn to cope during the year of facing unanswered questions.

Videos

Let's Explore a Forest. Washington, D.C.: National Geographic, 1994. 16 minutes. Grades 4 and up.
Explore the forest canopy of Tennessee's Great Smoky Mountains.

Let's Explore a Meadow. Washington, D.C.: National Geographic, 1994. 16 minutes. Grades 4 and up.
Explore a meadow near the Great Smoky Mountains of Tennessee.

Let's Explore a Wetland. Washington, D.C.: National Geographic, 1994. 17 minutes. Grades 4 and up.
Explore a swamp of a wildlife sanctuary in South Carolina.

The Lower South. Washington, D.C.: National Geographic, 1983. 26 minutes. Grades 4 and up.
Enjoy South Carolina, Arkansas, Alabama, Georgia, Mississippi, Louisiana, and Florida.

Steal Away: The Harriet Tubman Story. Washington, D.C.: National Geographic, 1997. 25 minutes. Grades 4 and up.
Provides the story of Harriet Tubman's 10 years of returning to the South to lead others to freedom.

The Upper South. Washington, D.C.: National Geographic, 1983. 26 minutes. Grades 4 and up.
Travel through North Carolina, Virginia, West Virginia, Kentucky, and Tennessee.

9
The Midwest and Prairies

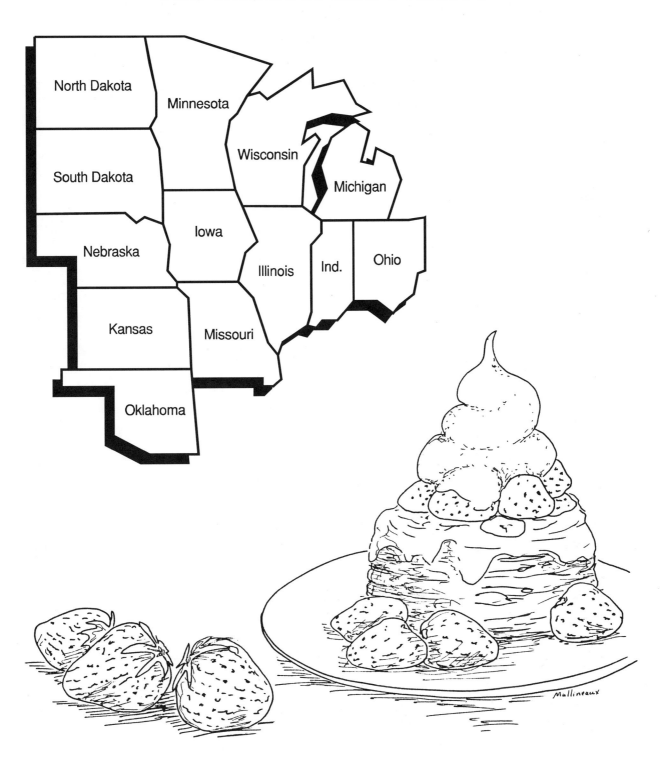

The Midwest and Prairies

Word List

- *Appelgebak, Anijsmelk*
- Butternuts
- Chinquapins, Crab apples
- Deviled eggs
- Eel
- Fruit soup
- Gooseberries
- *Hasenpfeffer*
- Immigrants
- Jerky
- *Kirschwasser*
- Lingonberry
- Muskellunge
- *Norske Jule kake*
- Opossum
- Pumpernickel, Papaw, Pemmican
- Quilting bees
- Rabbit
- Spicewood tea, Scones
- Trout
- Udders of buffalo
- Veal
- Walnuts
- X
- Yeast
- Zwieback

From *Cooking Up U.S. History*, Second Edition. © 1999 Suzanne I. Barchers and Patricia C. Marden. Teacher Ideas Press. (800) 237-6124.

CINNAMON ROLLS

Ingredients

2 packages dry yeast
¼ cup very warm water
    (110 to 115 degrees)
1 ¼ cups sugar
1 cup milk
3 tablespoons shortening
¾ teaspoon salt
1 egg, beaten

2 teaspoons vanilla
3 to 3 ½ cups flour
3 tablespoons melted butter
1 ½ teaspoons cinnamon
2 cups confectioner's sugar
1 tablespoon butter, softened
4 tablespoons milk

Steps

1. Dissolve yeast in warm water.
2. Add 1 teaspoon of the sugar.
3. Stir well.
4. Let yeast mixture stand.
5. Scald milk in medium saucepan.
6. Stir in shortening, salt, and ½ cup sugar.
7. Let mixture cool.
8. Stir in egg and vanilla.
9. Put 3 cups flour in a large bowl.
10. Add yeast mixture.
11. Add milk mixture.
12. Stir well until it forms a soft dough.
13. Put dough onto a floured board.
14. Knead for 10 minutes. Add more flour if dough is too sticky.
15. Grease a large bowl.
16. Put dough in bowl and roll it around to grease it.
17. Cover bowl and let rise in a warm place until doubled in size (about 1 hour).
18. Punch dough. Roll out on a floured board to ¼-inch thickness.
19. Brush dough with melted butter.
20. Mix remaining sugar with cinnamon and sprinkle over buttered dough. Roll dough up.
21. Using a sharp knife, cut slices 1 to 1 ½ inches thick.
22. Put slices down flat on a greased baking sheet.
23. Cover with a towel and let rise in a warm place until doubled in size (about 45 minutes).
24. Bake in a 325 degree oven for about 20 to 25 minutes or until slightly brown.
25. Beat confectioner's sugar in a medium bowl with softened butter and milk to make frosting.
26. While rolls are still warm, frost with confectioner's frosting.

Makes 9 to 12.

COFFEECAKE

Ingredients

5 cups flour
1 ½ teaspoons cinnamon
1 teaspoon allspice
1 teaspoon baking soda
¾ cup butter
2 ¼ cups brown sugar
3 eggs, beaten well
¾ cup molasses
1 cup cold coffee
1 ½ cups raisins

Steps

1. Put flour, cinnamon, allspice, and soda in a large bowl. Stir well.
2. Put butter and sugar in a medium bowl. Cream together.
3. Add eggs. Stir well.
4. Mix coffee and molasses in a small bowl.
5. Add ⅓ of the butter mixture to the flour mixture. Then add ⅓ of the coffee.
6. Continue with the rest of the butter and coffee. Stir well after each addition.
7. Add raisins and stir well.
8. Pour batter into a greased 11-by-14-inch baking pan.
9. Bake in a 275 degree oven for 30 to 40 minutes or until done.

Serves 10 to 12.

SWISS FONDUE

Ingredients

1 cup milk
¼ cup soft bread crumbs
½ pound Swiss cheese cut into cubes
1 tablespoon butter
½ teaspoon salt
3 eggs
French bread, cut in cubes

Steps

1. Mix milk, bread crumbs, cheese, butter, and salt in a large saucepan.
2. Cook over low heat until smooth, stirring constantly.
3. Remove from heat.
4. Separate egg yolks from egg whites.
5. Beat egg yolks.
6. Stir egg yolks into cheese mixture.
7. Beat egg whites until stiff.
8. Fold egg whites carefully into cheese mixture.
9. Pour mixture in a fondue pot. (Mixture may be reheated by baking in the oven.)
10. Dip chunks of bread into the fondue to serve.

Serves 4 to 6.

From *Cooking Up U.S. History*, Second Edition. © 1999 Suzanne I. Barchers and Patricia C. Marden. Teacher Ideas Press. (800) 237-6124.

CHICAGO DEEP-DISH PIZZA

Ingredients
1 package dry yeast
1 teaspoon sugar
1 cup very warm water (110 to 115 degrees)
3 cups flour
½ cup cornmeal
1 teaspoon salt
¼ cup salad oil
1 pound Italian sausage
1 28-ounce can pizza sauce
½ teaspoon Italian seasoning
1 pound shredded mozzarella cheese
4 tablespoons grated Parmesan cheese

Steps
1. Dissolve yeast in ¼ cup water.
2. Add sugar and stir well. Set aside.
3. In a large bowl combine 2 ½ cups flour, cornmeal, salt, oil, and remaining ¾ cup water. Stir well.
4. Stir in yeast mixture.
5. Put dough onto a floured board. Let rest 5 minutes.
6. Knead dough 10 minutes. Add the rest of the flour as needed.
7. Grease a large bowl.
8. Put dough in bowl and roll it around until it is greased.
9. Cover with plastic wrap and let rise in a warm place until doubled in size (about 1 to 2 hours).
10. Preheat oven to 475 degrees.
11. Punch dough down.
12. Oil a deep dish pizza pan or a 12-by-15-inch cake pan.
13. Press dough out to cover the bottom of the pan.
14. Let dough rise in a warm place for 30 minutes.
15. Crumble, cook, and drain the Italian sausage.
16. Spread pizza sauce over dough.
17. Sprinkle Italian seasoning, sausage, and shredded mozzarella cheese over sauce.
18. Sprinkle Parmesan cheese on top.
19. Bake 15 minutes.
20. Lower oven temperature to 375 degrees and bake 20 to 30 minutes more. Bottom of crust should be browned.

Serves 4.

PASTIES

Ingredients
4 cups flour
½ teaspoon salt
1 ⅔ cups shortening, softened
1 cup cold water
1 large potato
2 carrots
1 small onion
½ pound ground beef
½ pound ground pork
2 tablespoons dried parsley
1 teaspoon salt
¼ teaspoon pepper
2 tablespoons melted butter

Steps
1. Combine flour and salt in a large bowl.
2. Cut in the shortening with knives until it is crumbly.
3. Slowly stir in the water until it forms a sticky ball.
4. Flour a sheet of wax paper. Roll dough in a ball and wrap it in the wax paper.
5. Put dough in refrigerator for 1 hour.
6. Peel potato and chop into fine pieces. Put in a large bowl.
7. Peel carrots and chop into fine pieces. Add carrots to the potatoes.
8. Peel and chop the onion. Add onion to the potatoes and carrots.
9. Add ground beef, ground pork, parsley, salt, pepper, and melted butter to the potato mixture. Mix well.
10. Preheat oven to 350 degrees.
11. Divide dough into 4 to 6 equal parts, depending on the size of pasty you want.
12. Roll each piece out onto a floured board to a 6-to-9-inch circle.
13. Divide potato mixture evenly among the dough circles.
14. Place mixture in middle of each circle.
15. Fold both sides up, forming a half-moon shape. Press edges together.
16. Crimp sealed edges with a fork.
17. Put pasties on a greased cookie sheet.
18. Bake 1 hour and 15 minutes to 1 hour and 25 minutes or until browned and cooked through.

Makes 4 to 6.

CONEYS

Ingredients

1 pound ground beef
1 small onion, chopped
1 tablespoon mustard
2 tablespoons vinegar
2 tablespoons sugar
1 tablespoon water
½ teaspoon Worcestershire sauce

¼ teaspoon salt
¼ teaspoon Tabasco sauce
Ketchup
6 hot dogs
6 hot dog rolls
Shredded cheddar cheese, if desired

Steps

1. Crumble and cook ground beef in a large skillet over medium heat.
2. Add onion and cook until clear and soft.
3. Add mustard, vinegar, sugar, water, Worcestershire sauce, salt, and Tabasco sauce. Stir well.
4. Simmer meat mixture over low heat.
5. Add enough ketchup to flavor.
6. Simmer 1 hour.
7. Cook hot dogs in boiling water until done (about 10 minutes).
8. Put hot dogs in rolls and top with meat sauce. Add cheddar cheese if desired.

Serves 6.

FISH BALLS

Ingredients

½ pound cod fillets
2 ½ cups potatoes, peeled and cubed
1 tablespoon butter
1 beaten egg
¼ teaspoon pepper
¼ teaspoon salt
Butter for frying

Steps

1. Put fish and potatoes in a large saucepan and cover with water.
2. Boil until potatoes are almost soft.
3. Drain until nearly dry.
4. Mash mixture together.
5. Stir in butter, egg, pepper, and salt.
6. Beat until mixture is smooth.
7. Heat butter in large frying pan.
8. Form fish mixture into balls and fry in butter until well browned on all sides.

Serves 6.

ANGEL FOOD CAKE

Ingredients

10 eggs whites, at room temperature
¼ teaspoon salt
1 teaspoon cream of tartar
½ teaspoon almond extract

1 teaspoon vanilla extract
1 ½ cups sugar
1 cup flour

Steps

1.   Put the egg whites and salt in a large metal or glass bowl.
2.   Beat with an electric mixer on high until foamy.
3.   Add cream of tartar and beat until soft peaks form.
4.   Add almond and vanilla extracts. Mix well.
5.   Mix flour and sugar together in a small bowl.
6.   Add 2 tablespoons of the flour mixture to the egg whites. Fold in carefully using a wire whisk.
7.   Continue to fold in flour mixture 2 tablespoons at a time until it is all mixed in.
8.   Preheat oven to 325 degrees.
9.   Pour cake batter into a 10-inch ungreased tube pan.
10.   Bake for 50 minutes. Turn the oven off and leave cake in the oven for 10 more minutes.
11.   Remove pan from oven. Turn upside down until the cake cools.

Makes 1 cake.

STRAWBERRY SHORTCAKE

Ingredients

1 pint fresh strawberries
⅓ cup sugar
1 cup flour
2 teaspoons baking powder
¼ teaspoon salt

1 tablespoon sugar
4 tablespoons shortening
¼ cup milk
Heavy cream

Steps

1.   Hull and wash berries.
2.   Put berries in a medium-sized bowl. Chop into large pieces.
3.   Add sugar to taste. Stir well.
4.   Set berry mixture aside.
5.   Put flour, baking powder, salt, and sugar into a large bowl. Stir.
6.   Cut the shortening into the flour mixture until crumbly.
7.   Add milk. Stir until it becomes a stiff dough. Add milk if it becomes too dry.
8.   Pat dough onto a floured board to a ¾-inch thickness.
9.   Cut dough with a round cutter. Place on an ungreased baking sheet.
10.   Bake in a 400 degree oven for about 15 minutes or until browned.
11.   Split and butter warm shortcakes.
12.   Spoon berries over shortcakes.
13.   Top with heavy cream.

Serves 4 to 5.

DUTCH APPLE KUCHEN

Ingredients

2 cups flour
4 teaspoons baking powder
½ teaspoon salt
⅓ cup sugar
⅓ cup softened butter
1 egg

⅓ cup milk
5 sour apples
½ cup sugar
1 teaspoon cinnamon
3 tablespoons currants
Whipped cream

Steps

1. Stir together flour, baking powder, salt, and ⅓ cup sugar in a large mixing bowl.
2. Mix in butter and egg until mixture is crumbly.
3. Stir in milk until dough holds together.
4. Grease a 9-inch round cake pan.
5. Spread dough in pan.
6. Preheat oven to 350 degrees.
7. Peel, core, and slice apples.
8. Arrange apples in a pattern on top of the dough.
9. Mix ½ cup sugar and cinnamon.
10. Sprinkle sugar and cinnamon mixture over apples.
11. Sprinkle currants over apples.
12. Bake 25 to 30 minutes or until apples are tender and cake is done.
13. Serve with whipped cream on top.

Makes 1 cake.

SPRITZ COOKIES

Ingredients

1 cup softened butter
¾ cup sugar
1 egg
2 ¼ cups flour
½ teaspoon baking powder
¼ teaspoon salt
1 teaspoon vanilla extract

Steps

1. Cream shortening in a large mixing bowl.
2. Stir in sugar and egg. Mix well.
3. Add flour, baking powder, salt, and vanilla. Mix well.
4. Force dough through a cookie press onto an ungreased cookie sheet.
5. Bake at 375 degrees for 8 to 12 minutes or until cookies are slightly brown on the bottom.

Makes 4 ½ to 5 dozen.

CHERRY PIE

Ingredients

4 cups sour red cherries

⅔ cup sugar

2 ½ tablespoons flour

2 flat unbaked 9-inch pie pastries

Steps

1. Stone cherries (remove seeds). Save juice.
2. Line pie pan with pastry.
3. Put cherries and juice on top of pastry.
4. Sprinkle cherries with sugar and flour.
5. Cover with top crust.
6. Cut slits in top pastry.
7. Seal and crimp edges.
8. Bake in a 400 degree oven for 5 minutes.
9. Reduce heat to 350 degrees. Bake 40 more minutes until crust is light brown and juice bubbles up through slits.

Serves 6 to 8.

Library Links

Library Link 1:   Where does cinnamon come from?

Library Link 2:   According to tradition, what happens if a girl drops a chunk of bread into the fondue?

Library Link 3:   After the Civil War, Chicago became the most important meat marketing center in the world. What invention made mass production of meat possible?

Library Link 4:   Where did pasties originate?

Library Link 5:   How did frankfurters become known as hot dogs?

Library Link 6:   Cod are saltwater fish. What fish are both saltwater and freshwater fish?

Library Link 7:   Where was angel food cake first created?

Library Link 8:   What did the early settlers call strawberry shortcake?

Library Link 9:   How did Johnny Appleseed obtain his seeds?

Library Link 10:   Where does the name *spritz* come from and what does it mean?

Library Link 11:   What did the early settlers on the prairie often use for fuel?

Bibliography—The Midwest and Prairies

Nonfiction

Bial, Raymond. *Where Lincoln Walked.* New York: Walker, 1997. Grades 3 and up.
    Focusing on Lincoln's early years, the rich photographs enhance a fascinating overview of Lincoln's homes, schooling, and family life.

Conrad, Pam. *Prairie Visions: The Life and Times of Solomon Butcher.* New York: Harper-
    Collins, 1991. Grades 4 and up.
    Solomon Butcher decided to photograph Custer County, Nebraska, in the late 1800s and through the turn of the century. Conrad's text and his photographs describe life during this era.

McPherson, Stephanie Sammartino. *The Worker's Detective: A Story About Dr. Alice Hamilton.*
    Illustrated by Janet Schulz. Minneapolis, Minn.: Carolrhoda, 1992. Grades 4 and up.
    The story of this doctor, social worker, and activist's work in Chicago will inspire readers of all ages with the accomplishments one person can achieve.

Patent, Dorothy Hinshaw. *Prairies.* Photographs by William Nuñoz. New York: Holiday House,
    1996. Grades 3 and up.
    The plants and animals of the prairie, plus its harsh environment and preserves, are described through text and photographs.

Ross, Jim, and Paul Myers, editors. *Dear Oklahoma City, Get Well Soon: America's Children
    Reach Out to the People of Oklahoma.* New York: Walker, 1996. Grades 3 and up.
    In the wake of the bombing in Oklahoma City on April 19, 1995, many children opened their hearts through letters and drawings. This collection, accompanied by quotes from many of those involved in the rescue efforts, provides compelling reading about this tragic event.

Stanley, Jerry. *Children of the Dust Bowl: The True Story of the School at Weedpatch Camp.* New
    York: Crown, 1992. Grades 4 and up.
    For four years dry winds blew through western Kansas, eastern Colorado, the Oklahoma Panhandle, northeastern New Mexico, and northern Texas. Through compelling photographs, text, and maps, Stanley tells the story of these desperate years.

Fiction

Deaver, Julie Reece. *Chicago Blues.* New York: HarperCollins, 1995. Grades 6 and up.
    Lissa, a student in a Chicago art school, is forced to take over the care of her younger sister. In spite of the challenges of living in a big city with limited means, they discover that they can succeed until their mother can resume care for Marnie.

Fleischman, Paul. *The Borning Room.* New York: HarperCollins, 1991. Grades 5 and up.
    Georgina, born in the room where she lies dying, recalls the lives that have begun and ended in this room. Through her remembrances, the reader learns of life on an Ohio farm during the mid-1800s through the early 1900s.

———. *Seedfolks.* New York: HarperCollins, 1997. Grades 5 and up.
  A group of disparate urban dwellers in Cleveland come together to transform an abandoned lot into a garden.

Haddix, Margaret Peterson. *Running Out of Time.* New York: Simon & Schuster, 1995. Grades 5 and up.
  In Clifton, Indiana, where children are being stricken with diphtheria, it is 1840. Elsewhere the year is 1996. In this mix of historical and science fiction, a young boy must escape Clifton to get medical help.

Henry, Joanne Landers. *A Clearing in the Forest: A Story About a Real Settler Boy.* Illustrated by Charles Robinson. New York: Four Winds Press, 1992. Grades 3 and up.
  Elijah loves town life in Indianapolis in the 1830s. Based on the diaries of the Fletcher family, readers learn about the excitement of this period.

Hutchins, Hazel. *Tess.* Illustrated by Ruth Ohi. New York: Annick Press Ltd., 1995. Grades kindergarten and up.
  Tess lives on the prairie where life is hard. She and her brother even have to gather cow patties for fuel! When she saves a grumpy neighbor's dog from coyotes she makes a new friend.

Karr, Kathleen. *Gideon and the Mummy Professor.* New York: Farrar, Straus & Giroux, 1993. Grades 5 and up.
  Gideon assists his father as they travel down the Mississippi River with an Egyptian mummy.

Lawlor, Laurie. *Addie's Forever Friend.* Illustrated by Helen Cogancherry. Morton Grove, Ill.: Albert Whitman and Company, 1997. Grades 3 and up.
  Addie lives in Iowa, enjoying her friendship with Eleanor. But Eleanor is more daring than Addie. Addie worries about moving to Dakota and losing her best friend. The story provides a fine context for life in an early town. See other titles in this series: *Addie Across the Prairie, Addie's Dakota Winter,* and *Addie's Long Summer.*

Love, D. Anne. *Dakota Spring.* Illustrated by Ronald Himler. New York: Holiday House, 1995. Grades 2 and up.
  Caroline and her brother must run the Dakota farm when their father is injured.

MacBride, Roger Lea. *Little House on Rocky Ridge.* Illustrated by David Gilleece. New York: HarperCollins, 1993. Grades 3 and up.
  Seven-year-old Rose Wilder travels with her father and mother to their new life in Missouri.

———. *Little Town in the Ozarks.* Illustrated by David Gilleece. New York: HarperCollins, 1996. Grades 3 and up.
  After a fire on their farm, Rose Wilder and her family try to adjust to life in town.

MacLachlan, Patricia. *Skylark.* New York: HarperCollins, 1994. Grades 2 and up.
  When drought comes to the prairie, Sarah is forced to return to Maine with the children while Jacob stays behind.

————. *What You Know First.* Illustrations by Barry Moser. New York: HarperCollins, 1995.
        Grades 1 and up.
        When her family prepares to leave the farm, a young girl ponders all she has come to love
about the prairies.

Porter, Tracey. *Treasures in the Dust.* New York: HarperCollins, 1997. Grades 5 and up.
        The depression in Oklahoma is given life through the voices of two young friends, Annie and
Violet. When Annie leaves for California, their letter writing brings comfort and sustains their
friendship.

Rodríguez, Luis J. *América Is Her Name.* Illustrated by Carlos Vásquez. Willimantic, Conn.:
        Curbstone Press, 1997. Grades 3 and up. Preread.
        A Mixteca Indian from Oaxaca struggles to adjust to her new life in Chicago, where despair
and violence surround her. In spite of negative experiences at school, she finds solace in writing.

San Souci, Robert D. *Kate Shelley: Bound for Legend.* Illustrated by Max Ginsburg. New York:
        Dial, 1995. Grades 2 and up.
        Kate loves the railroad and has memorized the schedule of the trains that run near their farm.
When she realizes a train has crashed in a terrible storm, she knows that she must risk her life to
help the men. Based on a true story.

Sandburg, Carl. *Grassroots.* Illustrated by Wendell Minor. San Diego, Calif.: Harcourt Brace,
        1998. Grades 3 and up.
        Sandburg's poems in praise of the Midwest have been lovingly illustrated by Minor.

Thomas, Joyce Carol. *I Have Heard of a Land.* Illustrated by Floyd Cooper. New York: Harper-
        Collins, 1998. All ages.
        A young black woman dreams of settling on the free land in Oklahoma during the 1800s.

Turner, Ann. *Dakota Dugout.* New York: Macmillan, 1985. Grades 1 and up.
        Life for a family in a sod house is described including the killing winter, the summer
drought, and the unending isolation. Finally their existence improves, but the early years are remembered fondly.

Whelan, Gloria. *Once on This Island.* New York: HarperCollins, 1995. Grades 5 and up.
        Mary O'Shea's life on Mackinac Island is disrupted when she learns of the war between
America and England in 1812. As members of her family leave, she desperately hopes that peace
will bring her loved ones to the home she tries to preserve.

Willard, Nancy. *Cracked Corn and Snow Ice Cream: A Family Almanac.* Illustrated by Jane
        Dyer. San Diego, Calif.: Harcourt Brace, 1997. Grades 3 and up.
        This collection of dates, gardening advice, recipes, photographs, and illustrations provides a
rich glimpse of life in the Midwest during the early 1900s.

CD-ROM

The American Girls Premiere. Minneapolis, Minn.: The Learning Company, 1997. Grades 4 and up.
　　This multimedia theater production tool with characters from the American Girls books includes a focus on pioneering on the Minnesota prairie.

Videos

The Great Lakes States. Washington, D.C.: National Geographic, 1983. 25 minutes. Grades 4 and up.
　　Explores why Illinois, Indiana, Michigan, Wisconsin, and Ohio almost form an island.

The Heartland. Washington, D.C.: National Geographic, 1983. 25 minutes. Grades 4 and up.
　　Explores Minnesota, Iowa, Missouri, Kansas, Nebraska, North Dakota, and South Dakota.

Tallgrass Prairie: An American Story. Washington, D.C.: National Geographic, 1997. 28 minutes. Grades 6 and up.
　　Learn about the tallgrass prairie and the interaction of fire and bison on its development.

10
The Southwest

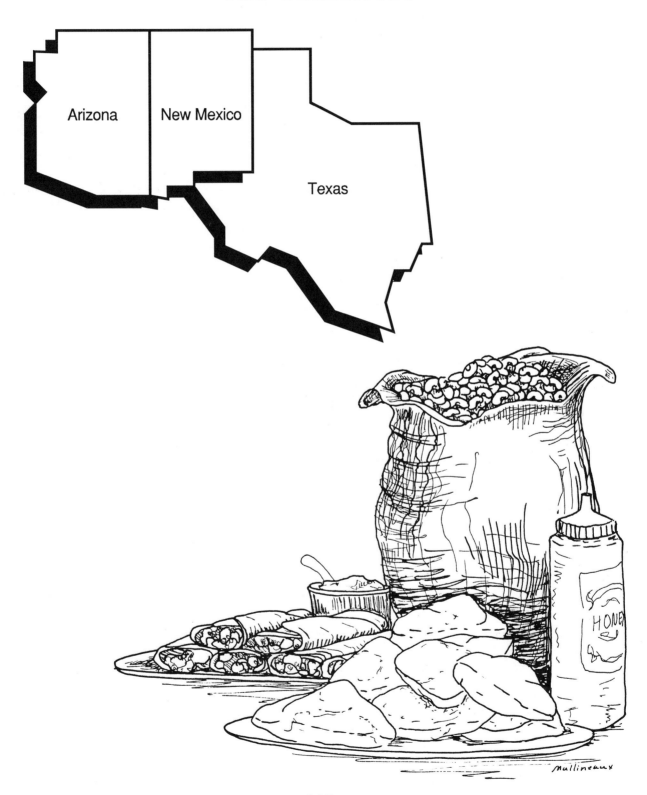

The Southwest

Word List

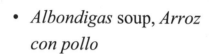

- *Albondigas* soup, *Arroz con pollo*
- Beans, Buffalo
- *Chorizo,* Chili con carne
- Dates
- Enchiladas
- *Frijoles*
- Garbanzo
- Hides
- Ices
- Jerky
- Kumquats
- Lemon
- *Mole, Masa*
- Nuts
- Olive
- Pine nuts, *Pinole,* Prickly pear
- Quesadillas
- Rice
- Spotted pup, Saffron
- Tortillas, Tamales
- Ugli fruit
- Vineyards
- Watermelon
- X
- Yams
- Zest

TORTILLAS

Ingredients
2 cups flour
1 teaspoon baking powder
2 teaspoons salt
2 tablespoons shortening, softened
½ cup water

Steps
1. Mix flour, baking powder, and salt in a large mixing bowl.
2. Cut in shortening.
3. Add water. Mix into a smooth dough with hands.
4. Let dough rest for 15 minutes in a covered bowl.
5. Pinch off a small piece of dough.
6. Roll dough into a small, thin circle.
7. Heat an ungreased frying pan over medium heat.
8. Put a circle of dough into the frying pan.
9. Cook until light brown on both sides.

Makes 8 to 10.

GUACAMOLE

Ingredients
2 ripe avocados, peeled and seeded
2 tomatoes, peeled and chopped
1 small onion, finely chopped
1 clove garlic, crushed
2 ½ tablespoons lemon juice
2 tablespoons chopped green chilies
¾ teaspoon salt

Steps
1. Mash all ingredients together in a large bowl. May be mixed in a blender.
2. Put in smaller bowl and cover.
3. Chill in refrigerator.
4. Serve with chips or as a spread.

Serves 2 to 4.

BURRITOS

Ingredients

1 ½ pounds cooked pork, cut into small pieces
3 small cans chicken broth
2 7-ounce cans green chilies, chopped
1 16-ounce can tomatoes, chopped
12 tortillas (see previous recipe)
2 16-ounce cans refried beans (or see following recipe)
4 tablespoons cornstarch
⅓ cup water
2 ½ cups grated cheddar cheese
3 tomatoes, chopped
2 ½ cups shredded lettuce

Steps

1. Put pork in a medium saucepan. Add chicken broth.
2. Cook over medium heat for 10 minutes.
3. Add chilies and canned tomatoes. Cook for 15 minutes. This is green chili.
4. Remove from heat.
5. Spread each tortilla with refried beans.
6. Strain green chili with a slotted spoon. Spread over refried beans.
7. Roll each tortilla up. Place in a 9-by-13-inch baking pan.
8. Bake uncovered in a 350 degree oven for 10 minutes or until hot.
9. Mix cornstarch and ⅓ cup water in a small bowl.
10. Bring remaining green chili mixture to a boil again over medium-high heat.
11. Slowly pour cornstarch mixture into chicken broth. Stir constantly until thickened.
12. Spoon green chili over burritos.
13. Sprinkle cheese, lettuce, and tomatoes over burritos.
14. Serve hot.

Serves 6.

REFRIED BEANS

Ingredients

1 pound dried pinto beans (2 cups)
1 small onion, diced
1 clove garlic, minced
½ pound salt pork or bacon, diced

1 teaspoon cumin
Salt and pepper (to taste)
Monterey Jack cheese, shredded

Steps

1. Place beans in a large saucepan. Cover with water.
2. Bring to a boil. Boil 5 minutes.
3. Remove from heat. Cover and let beans stand for 1 hour.
4. Drain beans. Put beans back in pan. Cover with water again.
5. Add onion, garlic, half of the pork, and cumin.
6. Bring to a boil. Boil until beans are tender (about 3 hours), adding water when needed to keep beans from drying.
7. Fry rest of pork until crisp in a large frying pan over medium heat.
8. Add beans to frying pan a little at a time, mashing as you add them.
9. Keep adding and mashing beans until they are the desired consistency.
10. Remove from heat and stir in salt and pepper to taste.
11. May be served warm with cheese sprinkled on top. Or use in other recipes.

Serves 6 to 8.

MEXICAN CORN

Ingredients

2 tablespoons olive oil
1 onion, finely chopped
2 cups tomato puree
3 tablespoons celery, finely chopped
1 ½ tablespoons chili powder
2 tablespoons butter
3 cups corn kernels
1 teaspoon salt
½ teaspoon pepper

Steps

1. Put oil in a large skillet over medium heat.
2. Add onion and sauté until slightly brown.
3. Add rest of ingredients. Stir well.
4. Remove from heat.
5. Butter a casserole dish. Pour all ingredients into it.
6. Bake for 30 minutes in a 350 degree oven.

Serves 6.

SOPA DE ARROZ

Ingredients
5 strips bacon
2 ½ tablespoons oil
3 cloves garlic, minced
1 small onion, finely chopped
2 cups rice
4 cups chicken bouillon
2 hard boiled eggs
Parsley for garnish

Steps
1. Put bacon, oil, garlic, and onion in a large skillet. Fry over medium-high heat until bacon and onion are browned.
2. Add rice and stir well.
3. Add chicken bouillon and bring to a boil.
4. Cover and lower heat so mixture simmers.
5. Simmer until rice is done, approximately 20 minutes.
6. Put into 4 bowls.
7. Top each with ½ hard boiled egg and parsley.

Serves 4.

HUEVOS RANCHEROS

Ingredients
10 eggs
2 tablespoons butter
5 tablespoons finely diced onion
5 tablespoons finely diced, roasted, and seeded red bell pepper
Salt and pepper

Steps
1. Break eggs into a medium bowl.
2. Beat eggs well.
3. Melt butter in a large skillet over medium heat.
4. Sauté onion in butter until lightly browned.
5. Turn heat down to low.
6. Add eggs and pepper and cook, stirring frequently, for about 4 minutes. Eggs should be done, but still creamy.
7. Serve with salt and pepper to taste.

Serves 4 to 5.

CHILE CON CARNE

Ingredients

1 pound ground beef
1 medium onion, chopped fine
1 clove garlic, chopped fine
2 small cans stewed tomatoes

2 small cans chili beans in chili sauce
1 teaspoon salt
½ teaspoon pepper
1 ½ teaspoons chili powder

Steps

1. In a large, deep skillet, fry ground beef over medium-high heat until browned and crumbly. Drain off grease.
2. Add onion and garlic. Cook until clear and soft.
3. Stir in tomatoes, chili beans, salt, pepper, and chili powder.
4. Simmer over low heat 45 minutes to 1 hour. Stir occasionally.

Serves 4 to 6.

TAMALE PIE

Ingredients

2 cups cornmeal
Water
2 pounds ground beef
1 clove garlic, finely chopped
¼ teaspoon oregano, crushed
1 tablespoon flour
1 ½ cups water
1 ½ cups pitted, ripe olives, finely chopped
1 large can stewed tomatoes
1 tablespoon red chili powder
2 cups Longhorn cheese, grated
1 cup Monterey Jack cheese, grated

Steps

1. Put cornmeal in a large saucepan. Cover with water.
2. Cook over medium heat, adding water when necessary, until cornmeal makes a thick mush (about ½ hour).
3. Put ground beef, garlic, and oregano in a large frying pan. Cook over medium heat until beef is cooked through.
4. Stir flour into the beef mixture. Mix well.
5. Add 1 ½ cups water to make a gravy. Stir well.
6. Stir in olives, tomatoes, and red chili powder. Simmer 15 minutes.
7. Add 1 cup Longhorn cheese to cooked mush. Stir.
8. Pour mush into a large casserole dish or 9-by-13-inch baking pan.
9. Layer the Monterey Jack and remaining Longhorn cheese and ground beef in the pan until they are used up, ending with cheese on top.
10. Bake at 350 degrees for 1 hour.

Serves 6 to 8.

TRAPPERS FRUIT

Ingredients

2 pounds dried apples
2 cups applesauce
4 tablespoons honey

⅓ cup chopped nuts
½ cup raisins
¼ cup cider

Steps

1. Put all ingredients in a large saucepan.
2. Cook over medium-low heat for 15 to 20 minutes. Stir often.
3. Remove from heat. Let cool before eating.

Serves 6 to 8.

CAPIROTADA

Ingredients

1 cup raisins
1 cup hot water
4 eggs
2 cups milk
½ pound brown sugar
1 ½ cups sliced apples
1 ½ teaspoons cinnamon
1 teaspoon nutmeg
3 slices dried or toasted bread
1 stick butter, melted
1 cup Longhorn cheese, grated

Steps

1. Put raisins in a small bowl and pour hot water over them.
2. Let sit for 5 minutes. Drain.
3. Put eggs in a large bowl. Beat well.
4. Add milk. Stir.
5. Add brown sugar. Mix well.
6. Stir in apples, cinnamon, and nutmeg.
7. Tear bread into small pieces. Add to milk and egg mixture.
8. Stir in melted butter.
9. Add raisins. Mix well.
10. Pour ½ of the milk and egg mixture into a 1 ½- to 2-quart casserole dish.
11. Sprinkle ½ of the cheese over it.
12. Pour the rest of the milk mixture into the casserole dish.
13. Sprinkle the rest of the cheese on top of it.
14. Bake in a 350 degree oven 45 minutes or until done in the middle.

Serves 4.

WO-JAPI

Ingredients

1 large (20-ounce) can blackberries
2 cups sugar
3 tablespoons flour

Water
1 teaspoon lemon juice

Steps

1. Drain blackberries. Save the juice.
2. Put blackberries and sugar in a medium saucepan.
3. Measure juice from blackberries. Add water to equal 2 cups.
4. Mix flour, juice, and water in a small bowl. Mix thoroughly.
5. Add flour mixture to berries and sugar.
6. Cook over medium-high heat until mixture boils. Stir frequently.
7. Turn heat down. Simmer slowly for 15 minutes.
8. Stir in lemon juice.
9. Chill before serving.

Serves 4 to 6.

BISCOCHITOS

Ingredients

3 eggs
1 cup shortening, softened
2 cups flour
1 ¾ cups sugar
2 tablespoons anise seed
2 tablespoons vanilla
4 tablespoons water
Cinnamon

Steps

1. Beat eggs well in a small bowl.
2. Cut in shortening with flour in a large bowl.
3. Mix sugar into flour and shortening.
4. Add eggs and anise seeds. Mix well.
5. Make mixture into a firm dough. Add more flour if needed.
6. Roll dough out onto a floured board about ½ inch thick.
7. Cut dough with cookie cutters. Place on cookie sheet.
8. Mix vanilla with water.
9. Rub vanilla mixture on tops of cookie. Sprinkle with cinnamon.
10. Bake in a 375 degree oven for 3 to 5 minutes or until slightly brown.
11. Serve warm.

Makes 3 to 4 dozen.

SOPAIPILLAS

Ingredients

4 cups flour
2 ½ teaspoons baking powder
2 teaspoons salt
1 tablespoon shortening, softened
1 ¼ cups water
Oil for deep fat frying
Honey

Steps

1. Mix flour, baking powder, and salt in a large mixing bowl.
2. Cut in shortening.
3. Add water and knead with hands until dough is smooth.
4. Put dough in a plastic bag and let stand for 2 hours.
5. Roll dough out very thin on a floured board.
6. Cut dough into small triangles.
7. Heat oil in a large saucepan to 375 degrees.
8. Drop triangles into hot oil. Fry until browned on both sides.
9. Drain triangles on paper towels.
10. Serve warm with honey.

Serves 10.

PINOLE

Ingredients

1 cup cornmeal
⅓ cup sugar
½ teaspoon cinnamon
¼ teaspoon nutmeg
3 cups milk

Steps

1. Spread cornmeal onto a cookie sheet.
2. Bake it in a 425 degree oven for 5 minutes, stirring it every two minutes.
3. Remove from oven. Cool.
4. Mix sugar, cinnamon, and nutmeg together.
5. Add sugar mixture to cornmeal. Mix well.
6. Pour cornmeal mixture into a large saucepan.
7. Stir milk in slowly.
8. Cook over medium heat for 15 minutes, stirring constantly, or until mixture is thickened.

Serves 4.

From *Cooking Up U.S. History*, Second Edition. © 1999 Suzanne I. Barchers and Patricia C. Marden. Teacher Ideas Press. (800) 237-6124.

Library Links

Library Link 1:   What two grains are tortillas commonly made from?

Library Link 2:   What Native American Indian tribes lived in the Southwest?

Library Link 3:   Name as many kinds of beans as you can.

Library Link 4:   What is the origin of chili con carne?

Library Link 5:   What are regular tamales wrapped in?

Library Link 6:   What is applejack?

Library Link 7:   Why did the Spanish call this dessert "spotted dog"?

Library Link 8:   What Native American Indian tribe favored *Wo-japi*?

Library Link 9:   Biscochitos are used for what holiday in what state?

Library Link 10:   Barbecues originated in the Southwest. What is the origin and meaning of the word *barbecue*?

Library Link 11:   *Pinole* is a combination of what two cultures?

Bibliography—The Southwest

Nonfiction

Ashabranner, Brent. *Born to the Land: An American Portrait.* Photographs by Paul Conklin. New York: G. P. Putnam's Sons, 1989. Grades 4 and up.
Though primarily about present day New Mexico, this story begins with pioneer days, providing insights into the challenges faced by any rural community.

Christian, Mary Blount. *Hats Are for Watering Horses: Why the Cowboy Dressed That Way.* Illustrated by Lyle L. Miller. Dallas, Tex.: Hendrick-Long, 1993. Grades 2 and up.
Everything the cowboy owned served a purpose. This intriguing book describes the functions of a cowboy's clothing.

Goodman, Susan E. *Stones, Bones, and Petroglyphs: Digging into Southwest Archaeology.* Photographs by Michael J. Doolittle. New York: Atheneum, 1998. Grades 4 and up.
Rich photographs and intriguing text describe the efforts of a group of eighth graders as they try to solve the mystery of the Ancestral Puebloan people, who moved away from the Mesa Verde region of Colorado around A.D. 1300.

Silver, Donald M. *One Small Square: Cactus Desert.* Illustrated by Patricia J. Wynne. New York: W. H. Freeman, 1995. Grades 4 and up.
Discover the challenges and joys of desert life in this fascinating, liberally illustrated resource.

Stanley, Jerry. *Children of the Dust Bowl: The True Story of the School at Weedpatch Camp.* New York: Crown, 1992. Grades 4 and up.
For four years dry winds blew through western Kansas, eastern Colorado, the Oklahoma Panhandle, northeastern New Mexico, and northern Texas. Through compelling photographs, text, and maps, Stanley tells the story of these desperate years.

Wallace, Marianne. *America's Deserts: Guide to Plants and Animals.* Golden, Colo.: Fulcrum, 1996. Grades 3 and up.
This colorful guide can serve as a field guide as well as a research tool.

Fiction

Buchanan, Ken, and Debby Buchanan. *It Rained on the Desert Today.* Illustrated by Libba Tracy. Flagstaff, Ariz.: Northland, 1994. Grades 1 and up.
Text and colorful illustrations demonstrate the beauty of the desert after the first rain of the season.

Córdova, Amy. *Abuelita's Heart.* New York: Simon & Schuster, 1997. Grades 2 and up.
A child walks through the southwestern desert with her grandmother, learning to appreciate its beauty before returning to the city. Includes a recipe for Abuelita's "Happiness Meal."

Finley, Mary Peace. *Soaring Eagle.* New York: Simon & Schuster, 1993. Grades 5 and up.

When Julio and his father leave to deliver a letter, his father is killed and Julio, blinded by snow, is left to survive in the southwest wilderness. Rescued by Cheyenne, he is forced to overcome his prejudices while learning his true identity.

Hobbs, Will. *Kokopelli's Flute.* New York: Simon & Schuster, 1995. Grades 4 and up.

Tepary and his dog love to explore the cave dwellings where he discovers a bone flute. Through the magic of the flute he discovers a mystery that only he can solve.

Holmes, Mary Z. *Cross of Gold.* Austin, Tex.: Raintree Steck-Vaughn, 1992. Grades 4 and up.

It is the year 1615 in New Mexico when a friar and a young boy meet. Their relationship helps determine the future of this area.

Johnston, Tony. *The Cowboy and the Black-Eyed Pea.* Illustrated by Warren Ludwig. New York: G. P. Putnam's Sons, 1992. Grades kindergarten and up.

When Farethee Well's father died, she knew she had to ensure that she married someone who could help her take care of her Texas spread. In a spin-off of "The Princess and the Pea," she tests suitors by placing a black-eyed-pea under their saddle blankets until she finds an appropriate mate.

————. *How Many Miles to Jacksonville?* Illustrated by Bart Forbes. New York: G. P. Putnam's Sons, 1996. Grades kindergarten and up.

When the train arrived in Jacksonville, the children rejoiced. Anyone who loves trains or simply smelling the creosote of the tracks will enjoy this delightful story.

London, Jonathan, and Lanny Pinola. *Fire Race: A Karuk Coyote Tale About How Fire Came to the People.* Illustrated by Sylvia Long. San Francisco: Chronicle Books, 1993. Grades kindergarten and up.

Wise Old Coyote decides to trick the Yellow Jacket sisters to capture fire. He convinces the other animals to help him, and after their success, they enjoy the fire, warm food, and stories.

Lowell, Susan. *The Three Little Javelinas.* Illustrated by Jim Harris. Flagstaff, Ariz.: Northland, 1992. Grades kindergarten and up.

Collared peccaries (javelinas), tumbleweeds, saguaro ribs, adobe bricks—and a wolf—star in this outlandish version of the Three Little Pigs set in the Southwest.

Stevens, Jan Romero. *Carlos and the Squash Plant.* Illustrated by Jeanne Arnold. Flagstaff, Ariz.: Northland, 1993. Grades kindergarten and up.

When Carlos refuses to wash his ears, a squash plants grows and grows! He tries to hide it with a hat, but finally has to give in and wash. Presented in Spanish and English.

Wesley, Valerie. *Freedom's Gifts: A Juneteenth Story.* Illustrated by Sharon Wilson. New York: Simon & Schuster, 1997. Grades 1 and up.

June looks forward to Juneteenth, the celebration of the freeing of the slaves in Texas, but she does not look forward to the arrival of her cousin Lillie from New York. After initial conflict, they both learn about the benefits of this special celebration.

Wisler, G. Clifton. *Caleb's Choice.* New York: Dutton, 1996. Grades 4 and up.
  When Caleb's family falls on hard times, he is sent to live with his grandmother in Texas. There he learns about superstitions and slavery issues, finding he must make some difficult choices.

———. *Jericho's Journey.* New York: Lodestar, 1993. Grades 4 and up.
  Jericho's journey to Texas with his family in 1852 presents exciting challenges and unexpected danger.

Kits

Southwest Treasure Box. Española, N. Mex.: Juniper Learning. (800-456-1776.)
  Includes student handbooks, 20 authentic primary source items, bulletin board kit, map, color photographs, and so forth.

Turquoise Language Arts Program. Española, N. Mex.: Juniper Learning. (800-456-1776.)
  Includes turquoise nuggets, *The Giant with Turquoise Heart* book, and the Cochiti pueblo turquoise legend in English and Spanish.

Videos

Let's Explore a Desert. Washington, D.C.: National Geographic, 1994. 17 minutes. Grades 4 and up.
  A naturalist and his nephew explore the Sonoran Desert of Arizona.

The Southwest. Washington, D.C.: National Geographic, 1983. 27 minutes. Grades 4 and up.
  Explore Texas, Oklahoma, Arizona, and New Mexico.

11
The West

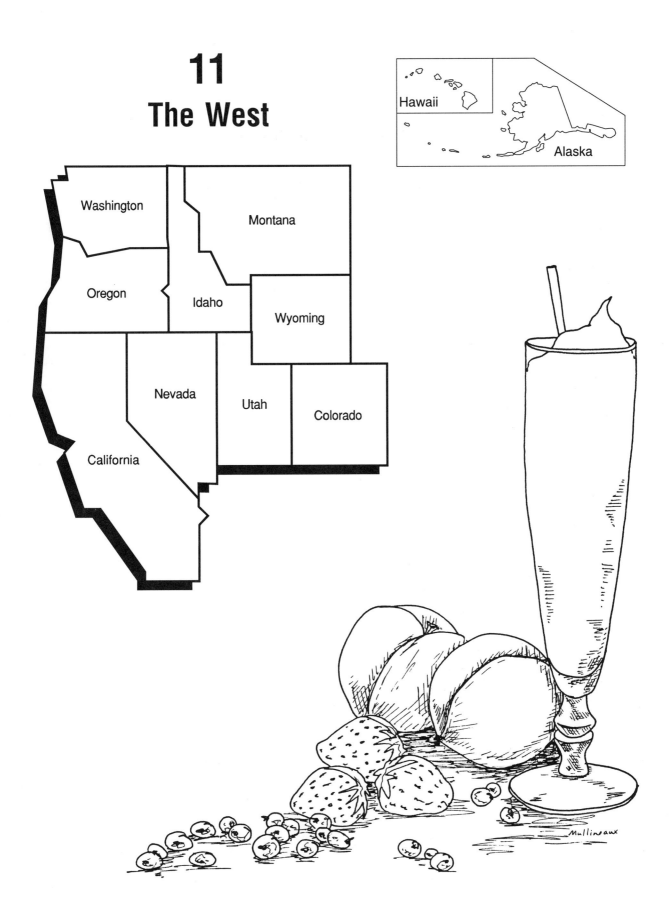

Hawaii

Alaska

Washington

Montana

Oregon

Idaho

Wyoming

Nevada

Utah

Colorado

California

Mullineaux

The West

Word List

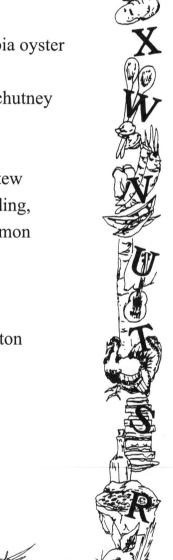

- Abalone, Alligator pears
- Bitterroot
- Codfish, *Cioppino*
- Dewberry
- Elk
- Filberts
- Geoduck
- Halibut, Hangtown fry
- *Imu*
- Johnnycake
- *Kava*
- Litchi nut, Luau,
  Loganberry
- Money-shell clams,
  Macadamia nut
- Nectarines
- *Opihi,* Olympia oyster
- Pigeon pie,
  Purple plum chutney
- Quail
- Razor clams,
  Red flannel stew
- Summer pudding,
  Sturgeon, Salmon
- Taro, turtle
- Ukelele
- Venison
- Waffle, Won ton
- X
- Youngberry
- Zucchini

WESTERN STEAK AND EGGS

Ingredients

2 6-ounce steaks
   (rib steaks with bone cut out)
1 ½ cups coarse salt
Water

2 tablespoons oil
1 ½ tablespoons butter
4 eggs
Butter

Steps

1. Put 2 large frying pans on the stove.
2. Heat 1 pan to medium-high.
3. Mix salt with enough water to make a thick paste.
4. Spread paste on one side of the steaks. Add oil to pan. Put steaks paste side down in the hot frying pan.
5. Spread the other side of the steaks with the rest of the paste.
6. Cook steaks on both sides until crusty and done.
7. When steaks are almost finished frying, heat other pan on medium-low heat and melt the butter.
8. Fry eggs to the stage you like to eat them.
9. Remove steaks from the pan. Scrape off all the salt coating.
10. Spread the top of steaks with butter. Serve immediately with eggs.

Serves 2.

DENVER OMELET

Ingredients

5 eggs
⅓ cup whole milk
½ teaspoon salt
⅛ teaspoon paprika
¼ teaspoon pepper
2 tablespoons butter

½ cup chopped green pepper
¼ cup chopped onion
⅔ cup chopped ham
1 cup grated cheese
   (Monterey Jack or cheddar)

Steps

1. Beat eggs with milk in a large mixing bowl. Add salt, paprika, and pepper. Stir well.
2. Put 1 tablespoon butter in omelet pan. Heat over medium-low heat.
3. In another large frying pan melt 1 tablespoon butter over medium heat. Add green pepper, onion, and ham. Cook for 5 minutes.
4. Pour egg mixture into omelet pan. Lift edges with a pancake turner and tilt pan to let uncooked egg run underneath.
5. When egg is almost cooked through, sprinkle green pepper, onion, and ham mixture over half of egg mixture. Sprinkle with cheese.
6. Fold other half over and serve hot.

Serves 4.

PECAN WAFFLES

Ingredients

1 cup pecan halves
2 cups flour
½ teaspoon salt
2 ½ teaspoons baking powder
½ teaspoon baking soda
2 teaspoons sugar
4 eggs, separated
1 cup milk
1 cup sour milk*
4 tablespoons melted butter
1 cup finely chopped pecans
¼ teaspoon cream of tartar
Butter
Syrup, warmed

Steps

1. Heat oven to 325 degrees.
2. Put pecan halves on a cookie sheet.
3. Bake pecans until browned (15 to 20 minutes), stirring several times.
4. Remove from oven and set aside.
5. Put flour, salt, baking powder, baking soda, and sugar in a large mixing bowl.
6. Beat egg yolks well.
7. Stir egg yolks, milk, sour milk, melted butter, and chopped pecans into flour mixture.
8. Put egg whites in a medium glass or metal bowl. Add cream of tartar. Beat eggs with an electric mixer until stiff.
9. Carefully fold egg whites into flour mixture.
10. Cook waffles in waffle iron until browned.
11. Serve with baked pecan halves on top and butter and syrup on the side.

* To make sour milk, add 1 tablespoon of vinegar or lemon juice to milk and let stand for 10 minutes.

Serves 4.

HAWAIIAN CHICKEN

Ingredients

1 chicken
2 cups chicken broth
1 ½ cups chopped, raw spinach
2 cups fresh, grated coconut

1 cup milk
Salt and pepper
2 cups cooked rice

Steps

1. Cut chicken into pieces and put in a heavy pot.
2. Pour broth over chicken.
3. Cover and simmer over low heat until chicken is tender, 30 to 45 minutes.
4. Add spinach and cook 5 minutes.
5. Put coconut in a medium saucepan and add milk.
6. Simmer over low heat for 5 minutes.
7. Remove from heat and drain, squeezing out all liquid.
8. Add the coconut mixture to the chicken. Bring to a boil.
9. Season with salt and pepper to taste.
10. Serve hot over rice.

Serves 4.

HAWAIIAN YAMS

Ingredients

3 tablespoons butter
4 tablespoons brown sugar
3 tablespoons cream
4 slices pineapple
2 cups mashed yams (canned or cooked fresh)
¼ cup milk
2 tablespoons melted butter
½ teaspoon salt

Steps

1. Put butter and brown sugar into a medium saucepan over low heat.
2. Stir in cream and continue to cook until bubbly.
3. Remove from heat.
4. Place pineapple slices in mixture, one at a time, turning over to coat both sides.
5. Place coated pineapple slices on 1 large or 4 small plates. Keep warm.
6. Add yams, milk, butter, and salt to the mixture in the saucepan.
7. Heat over medium heat, stirring well, until hot and fluffy.
8. Spoon yam mixture onto pineapple slices.
9. Serve warm.

Serves 4.

From *Cooking Up U.S. History*, Second Edition. © 1999 Suzanne I. Barchers and Patricia C. Marden. Teacher Ideas Press. (800) 237-6124.

CALIFORNIA DATE WALNUT BREAD

Ingredients

1 ½ cups pitted dates
1 cup sugar
1 cup water
½ cup shortening
2 eggs, beaten
2 cups flour

1 ½ teaspoons baking soda
½ teaspoon salt
¾ cup walnuts
2 teaspoons vanilla
Butter or cream cheese

Steps

1. Cut dates up into small pieces.
2. Put dates and sugar in a large mixing bowl.
3. Put water in a medium saucepan and bring to a boil.
4. Add shortening to water and continue boiling water until shortening is melted. Remove from heat.
5. Pour water and shortening over dates and sugar. Stir well until sugar is dissolved.
6. Add eggs, beating well.
7. Add flour, soda, and salt. Mix well.
8. Stir in walnuts and vanilla.
9. Put batter in a greased 9-x-5-inch loaf pan.
10. Bake at 325 degrees for 1 hour or until a toothpick inserted in the center comes out clean.
11. To serve, cut into thin slices. Top with butter or cream cheese.

Makes 1 loaf.

FRUIT SOUP

Ingredients

1 pound raisins
½ pound pitted prunes
½ pound currants
½ pound raspberries
6 apples, peeled, cored, and quartered

Juice of ½ lemon
Sugar
3 cinnamon sticks
2 tablespoons cornstarch
Water

Steps

1. Put raisins, prunes, currants, raspberries, apples, and lemon juice in a large saucepan.
2. Cover with water and simmer for 2 ½ to 3 hours or until apples are very soft.
3. Add sugar to taste. Stir well.
4. Add cinnamon sticks.
5. Mix cornstarch with ¼ cup water in a small bowl.
6. Stir slowly into simmering fruit mixture.
7. Cook 5 more minutes.
8. Remove cinnamon sticks.
9. Serve hot or cold as a first course or as a dessert.

Serves 4 to 6.

COBB SALAD

Ingredients

½ head iceberg lettuce
6 leaves romaine lettuce
2 stalks celery, chopped
1 avocado, chopped
1 large tomato, chopped
1 cooked boneless chicken breast, chopped
2 hard-boiled eggs, chopped
French, bleu cheese, or other salad dressing
2 ounces bleu cheese, crumbled
8 slices well done bacon, crumbled

Steps

1. Cut iceberg and romaine lettuce up into bite-sized pieces. Put in large salad bowl.
2. Add celery, avocado, tomato, chicken, and eggs. Stir together.
3. Add dressing. Mix well.
4. Crumble cheese and bacon on top.

Serves 2 to 3.

SALMON LOAF

Ingredients

1 large can salmon
1 egg, beaten
½ cup evaporated milk
¾ cup soft bread crumbs
½ teaspoon salt
¼ teaspoon paprika
¼ teaspoon pepper
1 tablespoon lemon juice
2 teaspoons Worcestershire sauce
1 tablespoon melted butter
3 tablespoons chopped parsley
2 tablespoons chopped onion
¼ cup chopped olives

Steps

1. Drain and flake salmon. Put it in a large bowl.
2. Add egg and milk to salmon. Stir lightly.
3. Add rest of ingredients. Mix well.
4. Place mixture in a greased loaf pan.
5. Bake in a 400 degree oven for 25 to 30 minutes or until cooked through.
6. May be served with a cheese or Hollandaise sauce.

Serves 4.

From *Cooking Up U.S. History*, Second Edition. © 1999 Suzanne I. Barchers and Patricia C. Marden. Teacher Ideas Press. (800) 237-6124.

CRAB LOUIS

Ingredients

1 cup mayonnaise
¼ cup heavy cream
¼ cup chili sauce
1 teaspoon Worcestershire sauce
¼ cup green pepper, chopped
¼ cup onion, chopped
2 tablespoons lemon juice
Salt and pepper to taste
Lettuce leaves
1 cup shredded lettuce
2 ½ cups cooked crab meat (Dungeness or Alaskan King)
2 hard-boiled eggs
Chopped parsley

Steps

1. In a large mixing bowl stir together mayonnaise, cream, chili sauce, Worcestershire sauce, green pepper, onion, lemon juice, salt, and pepper. Mix well into a smooth sauce.
2. Place lettuce leaves around the inside of salad bowls and add shredded lettuce.
3. Place cooked crab meat over shredded lettuce. Pour sauce over crab meat.
4. Slice hard-boiled eggs and place on top of sauce.
5. Sprinkle with parsley. Serve.

Serves 4.

FRESH COLORADO TROUT

Ingredients

½ pound bacon
1 onion, sliced thin
⅔ cup yellow cornmeal
½ cup flour

1 tablespoon salt
1 teaspoon pepper
2 freshly caught trout, cleaned

Steps

1. In a large frying pan, fry bacon over medium-high heat.
2. Remove bacon from pan.
3. Put onion in pan and fry in grease until soft.
4. Remove onion from pan.
5. Mix corn meal, flour, salt, and pepper in a medium bowl.
6. Coat fish well with corn meal mixture.
7. Fry fish in hot bacon grease over medium heat until browned on both sides.
8. Serve with bacon and onions sprinkled on top.

Serves 2.

CIOPPINO

Ingredients

2 tablespoons oil
4 tablespoons butter
1 small onion
3 sticks celery, chopped
1 carrot, chopped
½ green pepper, chopped
1 28-ounce can crushed tomatoes
1 tablespoon tomato paste
3 ½ cups water
3 teaspoons salt
½ teaspoon pepper
½ teaspoon thyme
4 bay leaves
2 pounds assorted seafood (halibut, cod, scallops, etc.)
1 pound medium shrimp, shelled and deveined
8 ounces crabmeat
2 tablespoons oil
2 tablespoons flour
4 tablespoons butter
1 teaspoon chopped garlic
½ cup water
½ cup chicken broth
1 dozen cherrystone clams
4 teaspoons chopped parsley

Steps

1. Put oil and butter in a large saucepan over medium-low heat.
2. Cook onion in oil and butter until soft.
3. Add celery, carrot, and pepper. Cook 5 minutes.
4. Add tomatoes, tomato paste, water, salt, pepper, thyme, and bay leaves. Cover.
5. Simmer 2 hours, stirring frequently.
6. Remove bay leaves.
7. Cut seafood into bite-sized pieces.
8. Dust assorted seafood, shrimp, and crabmeat with 2 tablespoons flour.
9. Put oil and butter in a large saucepan over medium-high heat.
10. Cook garlic in the oil and butter for 1 minute. Remove garlic from pan.
11. Add assorted seafood, shrimp, and crabmeat to heated oil and butter.
12. Cook over medium-high heat for 2 minutes until seafood is browned.
13. Add water and broth. Cook for 2 minutes.
14. Add tomato sauce to seafood mixture. Cook for 5 minutes over low heat.
15. Steam clams until shells open. Discard clams that do not open.
16. Place clams on top. Sprinkle with parsley. Serve.

Serves 6.

FILBERT CRESCENTS

Ingredients
1 cup confectioner's sugar
1 cup butter, softened
2 teaspoons vanilla
¼ teaspoon nutmeg
1 cup ground filberts
2 ½ cups flour
Confectioner's sugar for coating finished cookies

Steps
1. Sift confectioner's sugar.
2. Cream butter in a large bowl. Gradually add sugar to butter. Mix well.
3. Stir in vanilla, nutmeg, and filberts.
4. Stir in 1 ½ cups flour.
5. Work in the other cup of flour with hands.
6. Roll the dough in waxed paper. Chill 1 hour.
7. Remove dough from refrigerator.
8. Roll or shape dough into crescent shapes.
9. Put cookies on a greased cookie sheet.
10. Bake at 350 degrees 10 to 12 minutes or until lightly browned.
11. Remove from oven.
12. Dip cookies in confectioner's sugar while still hot.

Makes 4 to 5 dozen.

CALIFORNIA SMOOTHIE

Ingredients
4 bananas
2 cups strawberries
½ cup pitted dates
2 tablespoons bee pollen, optional
1 cup honey
4 cups fruit juice
2 cups crushed ice

Steps
1. Put banana, strawberries, and dates in the blender.
2. Mix on medium until smooth.
3. Add bee pollen and honey. Blend in.
4. Add juice and ice. Mix at high speed until well blended.
5. Serve immediately.

Makes 4 servings.

From *Cooking Up U.S. History*, Second Edition. © 1999 Suzanne I. Barchers and Patricia C. Marden. Teacher Ideas Press. (800) 237-6124.

Library Links

Library Link 1:   What method was used to preserve eggs in the 1800s?

Library Link 2:   What are some proverbs or sayings that mention eggs?

Library Link 3:   What is the source and meaning of the word *waffle*?

Library Link 4:   A popular California drink is a date milk shake. How is it prepared?

Library Link 5:   What are muscats?

Library Link 6:   Who were the Delmonico brothers? What effect did they have on the eating habits of Americans?

Library Link 7:   What river in the Northwest is known for its abundance of salmon?

Library Link 8:   What area in the West boasts the greatest number of Dungeness crabs? What geological features foster this type of crab?

Library Link 9:   What is a candlefish?

Library Link 10:   What does *cioppino* mean and where did it originate?

Library Link 11:   What nut is most similar to the filbert?

Library Link 12:   What causes variations in the taste of honey?

From *Cooking Up U.S. History*, Second Edition. © 1999 Suzanne I. Barchers and Patricia C. Marden. Teacher Ideas Press. (800) 237-6124.

Bibliography—The West

Nonfiction

Bernhard, Emery. *Reindeer*. Illustrated by Durga Bernhard. New York: Holiday House, 1994. Grades 1 and up.
The life of reindeer is described through simple text and softly colored illustrations.

Carlson, Laurie. *Westward Ho! An Activity Guide to the Wild West*. Chicago: Chicago Review Press, 1996. Grades 3 and up.
This resource is packed with an abundance of activities that will enhance any study of the West or westward expansion.

Christian, Mary Blount. *Hats Are for Watering Horses: Why the Cowboy Dressed That Way*. Illustrated by Lyle L. Miller. Dallas, Tex.: Hendrick-Long, 1993. Grades 2 and up.
Everything the cowboy owned served a purpose. This intriguing book describes the functions of a cowboy's clothing.

Ford, Douglas. *The Pacific Islanders*. New York: Chelsea House, 1989. Grades 5 and up.
Ford describes the histories and peoples of Hawaii, Polynesia, and Micronesia, and discusses their lives on the mainland. Many photographs provide insights into the people and their cultures.

Guiberson, Brenda Z. *Salmon Story*. New York: Holt, 1993. Grades 4 and up.
Salmon fishing has played an important role in the history of our country. Guiberson describes the history and challenges ahead for the industry.

Hoyt-Goldsmith, Diane. *Buffalo Days*. Photographs by Lawrence Migdale. New York: Holiday House, 1997. Grades 3 and up.
Through text and photographs, readers learn why buffalo remain important to the Crow people.

Johnson, Neil. *Jack Creek Cowboy*. New York: Dial, 1993. Grades 3 and up.
Johnson's text and photographs tell the story of Justin Whitlock's summer working the grazing area in the Wyoming mountains.

Kendall, Russ. *Eskimo Boy: Life in an Innpiaq Eskimo Village*. New York: Scholastic, 1992. Grades 2 and up.
Kendall's rich photographs and simple text describe Norman Kokeok's life in a small Alaskan village called Shishmaref.

Klein, James. *Gold Rush! The Young Prospector's Guide to Striking It Rich*. Illustrated by Michael Rohani. Berkeley, Calif.: Tricycle Press, 1998. Grades 4 and up.
Everyone who dreams of striking it rich will want to read this book. Chapters describe the history of the California Gold Rush, the people who mine for gold, places to search for gold, and how to talk like a miner.

Krensky, Stephen. *Striking It Rich: The Story of the California Gold Rush.* Illustrated by Anna DiVito. New York: Simon & Schuster, 1996. Grades 2 and up.
This easy, colorful chapter book provides a lively introduction to this fascinating period of western history.

Murphy, Virginia Reed, and James Reed. *Across the Plains in the Donner Party.* Edited by Karen Zeinert. North Haven, Conn.: Linnet Books, 1996. Grades 5 and up.
Drawn from the newspaper memoir of Virginia Reed and the letters by James Reed, Zeinert has compiled a history of the Donner expedition and the disastrous consequences of members' choices.

Stanley, Jerry. *Children of the Dust Bowl: The True Story of the School at Weedpatch Camp.* New York: Crown, 1992. Grades 4 and up.
For four years dry winds blew through western Kansas, eastern Colorado, the Oklahoma Panhandle, northeastern New Mexico, and northern Texas. Through compelling photographs, text, and maps, Stanley tells the story of these desperate years.

Wade, Linda R. *California: The Rush for Gold.* Vero Beach, Fla.: Rourke Enterprises, Inc., 1991. Grades 4 and up.
From Sutter's Sawmill to life in a mining town, readers are invited to learn about life during the gold rush. A final chapter gives advice for visiting gold country.

Wood, Ted. *Iditarod Dream: Dusty and His Sled Dogs Compete in Alaska's Jr. Iditarod.* New York: Walker and Company, 1996. Grades 3 and up.
Through informational text and vivid photographs, Wood describes Dusty's life in the community and his successful running in the Junior Iditarod.

Fiction

Beatty, Patricia. *The Nickel-Plated Beauty.* New York: Morrow, 1993. Grades 5 and up.
The seven Kimball children try to earn $27 to buy their mother a new stove in this story that highlights the simple life of the Pacific Northwest coast in the late 1800s.

Bunting, Eve. *Smoky Night.* Illustrated by David Diaz. San Diego, Calif.: Harcourt Brace, 1994. Grades 3 and up.
This Caldecott Medal winner explores the violence of the Los Angeles riots through a touching story and striking collages.

Cushman, Karen. *The Ballad of Lucy Whipple.* New York: HarperCollins, 1996. Grades 4 and up.
California Morning Whipple is so opposed to relocating in a California mining camp that she insists everyone call her Lucy. The book gives an accurate portrayal of life's challenges during the gold rush period.

George, Jean Craighead. *Julie's Wolf Pack.* Illustrated by Wendell Minor. New York: HarperCollins, 1997. Grades 5 and up.
In this follow-up to *Julie of the Wolves,* Kapu, the son of the wolf pack leader, Amaroq, must save his pack from disease and predators.

———. *Look to the North: A Wolf Pup Diary.* Illustrated by Lucia Washburn. New York: Harper-Collins, 1997. Grades 1 and up.
The lives of three wolf pups are described through diary entries and illustrations.

———. *One Day in the Alpine Tundra.* New York: HarperTrophy, 1984. Grades 3 and up.
Camping in the Tetons becomes treacherous for Johnny when a storm comes up.

Hobbs, Will. *Bearstone.* New York: Atheneum, 1989. Grades 5 and up.
A young Ute, sent to work for an old rancher, struggles to control his anger and determine where he belongs. With the rancher's patience and through meeting a challenge, he discovers his internal powers.

———. *Downriver.* New York: Atheneum, 1991. Grades 5 and up.
In this riveting tale, a group of youngsters decide to explore the Grand Canyon on their own, and face unexpected challenges with the river, rapids, and each other.

Karr, Kathleen. *Oregon, Sweet Oregon.* New York: HarperCollins, 1998. Grades 4 and up.
Phoebe Brown and other members of the Petticoat Party wagon train arrive in Oregon. The new life that mainly consists of hard work proves to be boring and Phoebe yearns for the excitement of the Oregon Trail.

Levitin, Sonia. *Boom Town.* Illustrated by Cat Bowman Smith. New York: Orchard Books, 1998. Grades 1 and up.
When the family moves to California to join their gold-mining father, they discover they must live in a town of tents and a few buildings. Gradually the town changes, thanks to the gumption and ingenuity of one smart young lady. See also the book that preceded this story, *Nine for California* (New York: Orchard Books, 1996).

Levy, Elizabeth. *Cleo and the Coyote.* Illustrated by Diana Bryer. New York: HarperCollins, 1996. Grades 1 and up.
When transplanted from the city to Utah, Cleo the mutt is scared by a coyote's howling. When they embark on an adventure together, they discover a lesson in love.

Love, D. Anne. *Bess's Log Cabin Quilt.* Illustrated by Ronald Himler. New York: Holiday House, 1995. Grades 4 and up.
Bess and her mother live in Oregon, passing the time by making quilts and farming until Pa comes back from bringing settlers out west. When Mama becomes ill and Pa's delay puts the farm at risk, Bess must win the quilting contest to raise money.

Porter, Tracey. *Treasures in the Dust.* New York: HarperCollins, 1997. Grades 4 and up.
Violet and Annie enjoy their lives in Oklahoma, in spite of living in the dustbowl during the depression. When Violet's family leaves to work the fields in California, the friendship continues until their separation ends.

Tunnell, Michael O. *Mailing May.* Illustrated by Ted Rand. New York: Greenwillow Books, 1997. Grades kindergarten and up.
  Imagine being mailed in a train 75 miles across Idaho to visit your grandmother! This actually happened to Charlotte May Pierstorff, whose story is charmingly depicted in this intriguing book.

Yep, Laurence. *American Dragons: Twenty-Five Asian American Voices.* New York: HarperCollins, 1993. Grades 5 and up.
  These short stories represent the writings of Asian Americans and their experiences.

———. *Dragon's Gate.* New York: HarperCollins, 1993. Grades 5 and up.
  It is after the Civil War, and the railroad developers begin to use Chinese workers. A young boy is sent to America to work the railroads, where he faces an adventure requiring courage to survive.

Audiotape

Ballad of Lucy Whipple. Performed by Christina Moore. Recorded Books.
  Karen Cushman's novel (above) is brought to life in this recording.

Kit

Rush for Gold Treasure Box. Española, N. Mex.: Juniper Learning. (800-456-1776.)
  Includes teacher's guide, student reproducibles, bulletin board kit, prospecting pans, gold flakes, balance scale, mineral samples, and so forth.

CD-ROM

Rush for Gold CD-ROM. Española, N. Mex.: Juniper Learning. (800-456-1776.)
  This interactive multimedia social studies program emphasizes reading skills and strategies.

Videos

Heritage of the Black West. Washington, D.C.: National Geographic, 1995. 25 minutes. Grades 4 and up.
  Discover the important role of African Americans in the settling of the West.

The Mountain States. Washington, D.C.: National Geographic, 1983. 25 minutes. Grades 4 and up.
  Travel through Idaho, Colorado, Utah, Montana, Nevada, and Wyoming.

The Pacific Coast States. Washington, D.C.: National Geographic, 1983. 25 minutes. Grades 4 and up.
  Explore California, Oregon, and Washington.

The Pacific Edge. Washington, D.C.: National Geographic, 1989. 20 minutes. Grades 4 and up.
Explore the fault lines and volcanoes of the West Coast.

The Rocky Mountains. Washington, D.C.: National Geographic, 1989. 20 minutes. Grades 4 and up.
Learn about the geology of the Rocky Mountains.

The West That Was. Washington, D.C.: National Geographic, 1996. 20 minutes. Grades 4 and up.
Discusses the fascinating life of the people along the Chisholm Trail.

The Western Dry Lands. Washington, D.C.: National Geographic, 1989. 20 minutes.
Explore the intermontane west.

Bibliography
Books About Food

The following books were particularly helpful for historical background information about foods of North America. Those that were written specifically for elementary school children are noted. Others books are intended for adults but may be used by mature readers or for reference.

Anderson, Jean. *Recipes from America's Restored Villages.* Illustrated by Martin Silverman. Garden City, N.Y.: Doubleday, 1975.
Anderson takes the reader on a culinary and historical tour of more than 40 restored villages across the United States. Recipes are included from past and present menus.

Giblin, James Cross. *From Hand to Mouth: Or, How We Invented Knives, Forks, Spoons, and Chopsticks and the Table Manners to Go with Them.* New York: Thomas Y. Crowell, 1987. Elementary.
Though not limited to North America, Giblin's account of the development of eating customs is an entertaining resource.

Herman, Judith, and Marguerite Shalett Herman. *The Cornucopia.* New York: Harper and Row, 1973.
The authors describe their book as "a kitchen entertainment and cookbook containing good reading and good cookery from more than 500 years of recipes, food lore, etc., as conceived and expounded by the great chefs and gourmets of the old and new worlds between the years 1390 and 1899."

Hintz, Martin. *Farewell, John Barleycorn: Prohibition in the United States.* Minneapolis, Minn.: Lerner, 1996. Intermediate.
Intermediate students and adults will be fascinated with this history of the role prohibition played in the United States during the 1920s.

Johnson, Sylvia A. *Tomatoes, Potatoes, Corn, and Beans: How the Foods of the Americas Changed Eating Around the World.* New York: Atheneum, 1997. Intermediate.
From maize to beans to peanuts to chocolate, Johnson provides a lively discussion of the roles these foods played in the development of eating patterns. Appropriate for intermediate students.

Kenda, Margaret, and Phyllis S. Williams. *Cooking Wizardry for Kids.* Hauppauge, N.Y.: Barron's, 1990.
More than 200 recipes, experiments, and creations can be enjoyed by students of all ages.

Penner, Lucille Recht. *Eating the Plates: A Pilgrim Book of Food and Manners*. New York: Macmillan, 1991. Intermediate.
Intermediate students can read how the Pilgrims hunted, gathered, grew, and prepared their food. The challenges of survival are clearly described.

Perl, Lila. *Hunter's Stew and Hangtown Fry: What Pioneer America Ate and Why*. Illustrated by Richard Cuffari. New York: Seabury Press, 1977. Intermediate.
Perl explores the role of food throughout the westward movement. She includes the adaptations of food made necessary by the conditions, as well as the contributions of immigrant groups. Selected recipes are included. This is suitable for intermediate students to read.

———. *Red-flannel Hash and Shoo-fly Pie*. Illustrated by Eric Carle. Cleveland, Ohio: The World, 1965. Intermediate.
Perl provides a regional and historical exploration of food in America. This is an excellent resource book for student researchers.

———. *Slumps, Grunts, and Snickerdoodles: What Colonial America Ate and Why*. Illustrated by Richard Cuffari. Boston: Houghton Mifflin, 1975. Intermediate.
Perl thoroughly discusses the importance of food in relation to colonial times. The key recipes of the period are included. This is suitable for intermediate students to read.

Rinzler, Carol Ann. *The Complete Book of Herbs, Spices and Condiments: From Garden to Kitchen to Medicine Chest*. New York: Holt, 1990.
For the reader interested in details about herbs, this is a must read.

Root, Waverly, and Richard de Rochemont. *Eating in America: A History*. New York: William Morrow, 1976.
This 500-page history should be the first source for anyone interested in learning about food in America. The authors have provided extensive information on virtually any aspect of the subject. No recipes are included.

Tannahill, Reay. *Food in History*. New York: Stein and Day, 1973.
This extensive book provides background information on food throughout the world from prehistoric days to the present. Though not specific to North America, the role of food in the New World is included. No recipes are included.

Visser, Margaret. *Much Depends on Dinner: The Extraordinary History and Mythology, Allure and Obsessions, Perils and Taboos of an Ordinary Meal*. New York: Grove Press, 1986.
Visser uses an ordinary meal of corn, butter, chicken, rice, salad with lemon juice and oil, and ice cream and delves into the history, issues, and practices surrounding each item.

Williams, Barbara. *Cornzapoppin'! Popcorn Recipes and Party Ideas for All Occasions*. Photographs by Royce L. Bair. New York: Holt, Rinehart & Winston, 1976.
Along with recipes and projects using popcorn, Williams provides a brief, fascinating history of popcorn in America.

Appendix A
Answers to Library Links

Chapter One: The Native American Indians

1. *Pawcohiccora* is the Virginia Native American Indian name for hickory nut.

2. Peanut butter, peanut oil, soap, face powder, shampoo, feed for cattle and pigs. The shells are used for plastics, wallboard, linoleum, and polishes.

3. Nuts were ground with stones.

4. Pemmican was carried in packets made of animal skin.

5. Beans were found in objects dating from 5000 B.C. excavated in Mexican caves.

6. Corn began as a wild grass.

7. Diggings in Mexico City revealed evidence of corn grains 60,000 to 80,000 years old.

8. Wild rice, which was not truly rice, was found near the Great Lakes. It grew in water and was called Indian rice or water oats by the settlers.

9. Sukquttahash, msakwitash, and m'sick-quotash are examples of Native American Indian spellings of succotash.

10. Answers will vary. Many tribes had well-defined table manners and included prayer before meals and formal thanks at the end of meals. In some tribes the husband waited on the guests. Plains Indians brought their own dishes with them and took them home for washing.

11. Answers will vary. The Native Americans were sophisticated farmers. They developed many varieties of beans and corn. They planted efficiently, knowing what vegetables to plant together to maximize the use of the soil without depleting it.

12. Native Americans would put a whole ear on a stick and hold it over the fire. They would also throw loose kernels into the fire, and when the kernels burst they would pop out of the fire. They would also heat a clay pot by pouring hot sand into it and putting it over the fire. When it was hot they would remove the pot, pour the popcorn into the hot sand, and stir it with a stick. The popcorn would pop to the top for eating.

From *Cooking Up U.S. History*, Second Edition. © 1999 Suzanne I. Barchers and Patricia C. Marden. Teacher Ideas Press. (800) 237-6124.

Chapter Two: The Colonial Period

1.   Oats are a cereal grass. They were used for food and to feed horses. Oats were important as horse feed because horses allowed the colonists to hunt and travel.

2.   Hasty pudding was made easily and quickly from cornmeal mush, a common item. Many children ate this as a quick supper.

3.   The Native American Indian word for corn is *maize.* Corn is a cereal plant and was introduced to the Pilgrims by the Native American Indians. The climate in England was not conducive to the growth of corn.

4.   Pilgrims dried the corn before grinding it into a coarse powder with a stone or wooden mortar and pestle. They used cornmeal because it was more plentiful.

5.   Life was basic. Their diet was a mix of English and Indian foods. The colonists primarily ate game birds, pork, and chicken for meat. They ate corn flour rather than wheat flour. They had little sugar or molasses for many years. They had to rely on what was readily available to them in America.

6.   The Pilgrims used dark beers and ales as sweeteners.

7.   The Dutch Colonists brought ole kooks to the colonies.

8.   Answers will vary.

9.   The bean plant is a legume. Other legumes are peanuts and coffee beans. Legumes could be dried for later use, as they endured long storage periods.

10.   Squash is harvested primarily in late summer and fall. The success of the harvest determined the amount of food the colonist would have during the next year.

11.   Clam chowder is well known. Chowders are popular on the coasts because of the availability of clams and fish.

12.   The Pilgrims would have to dry the corn and beans for winter use. They would then have to soak them in water before making succotash.

13.   The Pilgrims learned about pumpkins from the Native American Indians. Some examples of literary pumpkins are "Peter, Peter, Pumpkin Eater," *The Vanishing Pumpkin* by Tomie dePaola, and various Halloween stories.

14.   A quill is a feather from the tail of a large bird, such as a turkey. A section of the end was sliced off, sliced again to shape it, and then split.

15.   Early Americans used cut up linen rags that were washed and boiled with lye until the cloth had disintegrated. The lye was washed away and the remaining mass was reduced to pulp. A mold was dipped into the mass. For paper-making directions for children, see *Paper by Kids* by Arnold E. Grummer (Minneapolis, Minn.: Dillon Press, 1980).

16.   Answers will vary.

17.   Bees secrete wax, which was used for candles. Sheep provided tallow. Good candles could be made from the wax of bayberries.

18.   Molds were made by blacksmiths. Most candles were dipped because molds were unavailable until artisans were able to set up shop. Molds were made of tin or sometimes pewter. Eventually traveling chandlers, or candlemakers, brought large molds to a house and made up a family's stock.

19.   Answers will vary.

Chapter Three: Revolutionary War

1. "Sap's rising" means that the sap is moving through the trees. Actually the sap moves every direction, not just up.

2. Most spices were imported, and many new lands were discovered in the quest of finding spices. Spices were used in meat dishes to disguise the taste of the often spoiled meat.

3. Sweet potatoes are grown on a climbing vine in warmer climates. White potatoes grow underground. They were used because of their availability and appealing taste.

4. They cooked over open fires in black pots or in crude ovens. Sometimes a cake might be burned on one end and raw on the other end. They might try to bake by putting hot stones on top of a covered pot to distribute the heat more evenly.

5. Answers will vary. A pudding stone is a conglomerate.

6. A pudding cap is a padded cap worn by toddlers to protect their brains from turning into pudding if they fall.

7. Pies for company were kept in a chest. The word chess is thought to be a form of *chest,* indicating that the pie was kept in a chest until needed.

8. Suet.

9. A pound cake was made by actually weighing items. Eggs were smaller and the number needed for a cake would vary depending on size. Sugar had to be pounded out from a loaf or cone. Flour was coarse and very heavy.
   The tea parties were "tealess" to protest the British tax on tea.

10. "Little Miss Muffet." The first cows were brought in the early 1600s. Some reports state that they were brought to the Jamestown Colony in 1611. Others state that they arrived in 1624.

11. Strawberries, blueberries, blackberries, raspberries, elderberries, and currants.

12. John Chapman was born in Massachusetts in 1774. He began planting seeds in 1799 and traveled for 40 years, planting and tending his trees.

13. After the dinner women might rest while the men went to separate rooms to smoke, play cards, or converse. Musicians might play in a small orchestra or on a harpsichord or pianoforte. Guests would dance a gigue or minuet.

Chapter Four: Westward Expansion

1. Leather britches beans were made with green beans or pole beans that were dried in the sun for several days. When dried, they were soaked in cold water overnight and then cooked with salt pork or fatback till soft.

2. Prospectors were called sourdoughs because they often carried a pot with a pinch of sourdough in it. Their staples were beans, pork, and sourdough or baking soda biscuits.

3. Sourdough originated in Egypt, more than 6,000 years ago. It was the only way of leavening bread.

4. Modern technology made yeast, baking soda, and baking powder readily available, and sourdough was no longer needed to leaven bread.

5. Baking soda was called *saleratus*.

6. Corn was removed from the cob and dried in the sun.

7. *Frijoles* is the Mexican name for beans. The word *pinto* means "spotted."

8. Answers will vary.

9. Tomatoes originated in South America and were taken to Europe, where they were used as an ornamental plant for 200 years. They were brought back to America in the early 1800s. Many people thought tomatoes were poisonous or caused cancer.

10. Cranberries grow in cool, wet, sandy areas called bogs. Bogs are found in the Northeast and Northwest, near the coasts.

Chapter Five: The Civil War

1. Gail Borden worked hard at preserving foods, wanting to provide food that would travel. His factory was commandeered by the government to produce condensed milk for the soldiers. The soldiers then became proponents of the product, thus ensuring its continued use after the war.

2. Holes were added to dough nuts at the turn of the century (1900).

3. Potatoes came to Spain from Peru and were brought to Virginia by the colonists.

4. Weevils are a slim brown bug, $\frac{1}{8}$ of an inch in length. They would bore through hardtack.

5. The Homestead Act provided virtually free and formerly untilled land to would-be farmers. The abundance of food that subsequently became available benefited both the North and Europe.

6. In brief, the North had available an abundance of land, made available and fruitful through the Homestead Act. The soil of the South was exhausted through the planting of cotton and tobacco. When the plantations were converted to food production, the harvests were disappointing.

7. Sherman devastated the food supplies and crops as he swept through the South. When the war was ended, one of the first acts of the government was to rush food to the Confederate troops.

8. Ginger was imported from Jamaica, India, and the African countries of Sierra Leone and Nigeria.

9. Slaves baked hoe cake on a hoe over a small fire.

10. Approximately three shillings.

11. The cacao bean was dried and roasted over a fire. It was pounded into a powder. Sometimes sugar or other spices were added.

12. Other coffee substitutes were parched corn, peanuts, chicory, sweet potatoes, and rye.

Chapter Six: The Northeast

1. The bilberry is an English shrub that bears fruit that is very similar to blueberries. The colonists often confused them. The species is *Vaccinium.*

2. Oliver Evans began producing bolted flour in his watermill in the 1780s, and the use of flour became common by the 1830s.

3. The fat of pigs would be rendered for lard that was used for frying and for soap.

4. Bivalved means the two shells are hinged together.

5. The cherrystone clam is larger.

6. Coon oysters are mollusks about two inches long. They are so small that they are difficult to obtain in large quantities. They are favored by raccoons, thus the name of coon oysters.

7. Hash means something that is a jumble. It also means something that has been worked over.

8. Examples of clam types are pompano or coquina, littleneck, cherrystone, butter, razor, geoduck, and Ipswich.

9. The edible part of the beet that is included in this recipe (page 89) is the root. The leaves can be served in a salad.

10. Cranberries were first called crane berries because the shape of the blossom was like the head of a crane. It was shortened to cranberries later.

11. To "dowdy" means to cut up, as the crust is cut up after the first round of baking. A pandowdy has come to be known as a deep-dish pudding or pie made of apples.

12. The pumpkin plants helped keep down the weeds.

Chapter Seven: The Mid-Atlantic States

1. In addition to rye, corn, wheat, and buckwheat are grown in Pennsylvania.

2. The first commercial pretzel bakeries were established in the 1860s.

3. Matzo balls are eaten by Jews during the Feast of Passover.

4. Maryland wraps around the Chesapeake Bay, providing an abundance of shoreline and access to oyster beds.

5. Soft-shell crabs have recently shed their shells and have not grown a larger shell yet.

6. Holstein cows are used now because they produce about twice as much milk.

7. The name may have come from the Dutch word *snekrad,* meaning snail wheel, a wheel in clockworks. Another possible source is the German word *schnecke,* meaning snail and referring to the pinwheel shape.

8. The sweet sticky molasses at the top of the pie attracted flies and they had to be shooed away.

9. Zwieback is a kind of rusk or finger-shaped dry or toasted cake.

10. Henry Hudson.

11. Hex signs are thought to ward off evil spirits.

12. Dolly Madison (1809).

Chapter Eight: The Southeast

1. Grits were usually served with ham at breakfast.

2. Grits come from hominy that is ground into coarse meal.

3. A popular theory, though unproven, is that hush puppies got their name when a southern black cook would throw a bit of one to a barking puppy, calling, "Hush, puppy."

4. "Mama's Little Baby Loves Short'nin' Bread."

5. Louisiana.

6. Stack cakes were wedding cakes. Guests would bring layers and stack them. It was said that the taller the finished stack, the more popular the bride.

7. The Zuni made dumplings of blue cornmeal, called blue marbles.

8. King Henry VIII.

9. Americans eat about 250,000 tons of peanut butter each year.

10. To make candied fruit, boil ¾ cup sugar and ¼ cup water to soft-ball stage (236 degrees). Dip fruit in the syrup and dry on baking sheet.

Chapter Nine: The Midwest and Prairies

1. True cinnamon is from the bark of a tree from Sri Lanka and the Malabar Coast. A similar bark from Saigon is used for cassia cinnamon.

2. When a girl drops a chunk of bread into the fondue, the men may kiss her.

3. The refrigerated railroad car allowed the transportation of cut meat without spoilage.

4. Pasties originally came from Cornwall.

5. T. A. Dorgan, a cartoonist, drew a frankfurter with thick legs and a head, which became known as a hot dog.

6. Eel, elver, and shad are sea or freshwater fish, depending on their age or season.

7. Angel food cake originated in St. Louis, Missouri.

8. The early settlers called this dessert strawberry bread.

9. Johhny Appleseed obtained his seeds from cider presses in western Pennsylvania.

10. *Spritz* is a German word and means "to squirt."

11. The early settlers often used dried buffalo chips for fuel.

Chapter Ten: The Southwest

1.   Tortillas are made from corn and wheat.

2.   Pueblos, Hopis, Zunis, Comanches, Kiowas, Apaches, and Navajos lived in the Southwest.

3.   Types of beans include broad, black, turtle, cranberry, scarlet runner, red, kidney, black-eyed peas or beans, chick peas or garbanzos, soy, flageolets, adzuki, pinto, and cowpeas or Mexican frijoles.

4.   Chili con carne is believed to have been created in San Antonio, Texas, in the late 1800s.

5.   Tamales are wrapped in cornhusks.

6.   Applejack is distilled cider.

7.   Sometimes called "sopa" in New Mexico, the Spanish called it "spotted dog" because of the raisins in it.

8.   The Sioux Indians enjoyed *Wo-Japi.*

9.   Biscochitos are a popular Christmas cookie of New Mexico.

10. *Barbecue* came from the Spanish word *barbacoa,* meaning a framework of sticks.

11. *Pinole* is a Mexican Native American Indian beverage.

Chapter Eleven: The West

1. Eggs were preserved in the 1800s by immersing them in a water-and-lime solution or greasing them with melted mutton fat and storing them in a box of bran.

2. Answers will vary. Examples follow: "A kiss without a moustache is like an egg without salt" (old Spanish saying). "No wonder, child, we prize the hen, whose egg is mightier than the pen" (Oliver Herford). "Don't put all your eggs in one basket."

3. *Waffle* is a German word that means "weave" or "honeycomb."

4. Blend ¾ cup chopped dates and ½ cup milk in a blender until smooth. Add a pint of ice cream and ½ cup milk. Blend and serve.

5. Muscats are white raisins.

6. The Delmonico brothers opened a restaurant in New York City. They popularized the eating of salads by introducing endive, eggplant, and other unusual foods.

7. The Columbia River, between Oregon and Washington, has an abundance of salmon.

8. Puget Sound, Washington, offers more than 200 miles of coast that has a milder climate, which is conducive to Dungeness crab.

9. A candlefish is an oily fish that, when dried, can be lit and burned as a candle.

10. *Cioppino* originated on the San Francisco wharves, meaning to "chip in" to the stew kettle.

11. The hazelnut is similar to the filbert.

12. The taste of honey is affected by the soil, climate, and nearby flowers, trees, and bushes visited by the bees.

Appendix B
Measurements

How to Measure Accurately

Flour
Dip measuring cup into flour. Level off extra with a knife.

Sugar (granulated or confectioner's)
Spoon into a measuring cup. Level off with a knife.

Brown sugar
Pack brown sugar into a measuring cup. It should hold its shape when turned out of the cup.

Shortening
Use a spatula or scraper to pack it into a measuring cup. Level off with a knife.

Liquids
Pour into cup. A glass liquid measuring cup allows extra room at the top, preventing spilling.

Nuts, coconut, bread crumbs, cheese, etc.
Pack measuring cup lightly until full.

Spices, baking powder, salt, etc.
Stir. Fill measuring spoon and level off with a knife.

Measuring Equivalents

Dash	=	less than $\frac{1}{8}$ teaspoon
3 teaspoons	=	1 tablespoon
4 tablespoons	=	$\frac{1}{4}$ cup
5 $\frac{1}{3}$ tablespoons	=	$\frac{1}{3}$ cup
8 tablespoons	=	$\frac{1}{2}$ cup
10 $\frac{2}{3}$ tablespoons	=	$\frac{2}{3}$ cup
12 tablespoons	=	$\frac{3}{4}$ cup
16 tablespoons	=	1 cup
1 cup	=	$\frac{1}{2}$ pint
2 cup	=	1 pint
2 pints (4 cups)	=	1 quart

Butter

4 sticks = 1 pound = 2 cups

1 stick = $\frac{1}{4}$ pound = $\frac{1}{2}$ cup

$\frac{1}{2}$ stick = $\frac{1}{8}$ pound = $\frac{1}{4}$ cup

$\frac{1}{8}$ stick = 1 tablespoon

Eggs

Whole Medium	Whites	Yolks
1 = $\frac{1}{4}$ cup	2 = $\frac{1}{4}$ cup	3 = $\frac{1}{4}$ cup
2 = $\frac{1}{3}$–$\frac{1}{2}$ cup	3 = $\frac{3}{8}$ cup	4 = $\frac{1}{3}$ cup
3 = $\frac{1}{2}$–$\frac{2}{3}$ cup	4 = $\frac{1}{2}$ cup	5 = $\frac{3}{8}$ cup
4 = $\frac{2}{3}$–1 cup	5 = $\frac{2}{3}$ cup	6 = $\frac{1}{2}$ cup

Appendix C
Altitude Adjustments

Cakes:

At high elevations up to 3,000 feet:

        Raise the baking temperature about 25 degrees.
        Underbeat the eggs.

At elevations above 3,000 feet:

        Raise the baking temperature about 25 degrees.
        Reduce the double-acting baking powder or baking soda by $\frac{1}{8}$ teaspoon for each teaspoon called for in the recipe.
        Underbeat the eggs.

At 5,000 feet:

        Raise the baking temperature about 25 degrees.
        Reduce the double-acting baking powder or baking soda by $\frac{1}{4}$ teaspoon for each teaspoon called for in the recipe.
        Underbeat the eggs.
        Decrease sugar 1 to 2 tablespoons for each cup.
        Increase liquid 2 to 3 tablespoons for each cup.

For all high altitudes:

        Grease and flour all baking pans well. Cakes tend to stick.

Water:

Boiling temperatures (Fahrenheit)

Sea level	212 degrees
2,000 feet	208 degrees
5,000 feet	203 degrees
7,500 feet	198 degrees

From *Cooking Up U.S. History*, Second Edition. © 1999 Suzanne I. Barchers and Patricia C. Marden. Teacher Ideas Press. (800) 237-6124.

Candy:

For each increase of 500 feet above sea level, cook candy syrups 1 degree lower than indicated in the recipes.

Breads:

Reduce the baking soda or baking powder by ¼.

Glossary of Cooking Terms

Bake. To cook in an oven.

Beat. To mix with vigorous over and under motions with a spoon, whip, or beater.

Blend. To mix thoroughly.

Boil. To cook liquid until bubbles break on the surface.

Chill. To allow to become thoroughly cold, usually by placing in a refrigerator.

Chop. To cut in fine or coarse pieces with a knife.

Coat. To cover with thin film such as with flour, crumbs, or sugar.

Cool. To allow to cool to room temperature.

Core. To remove the core of a fruit.

Cream. To work shortening and sugar against the side of a bowl with a spoon or to beat with a mixer until thoroughly blended and creamy.

Cut in. To mix shortening into flour using a pastry blender, fork, or two knives.

Dice. To cut into small (about $\frac{1}{4}$-inch) cubes.

Fold in. To cut through the center of batter with a spoon, scraper, or spatula, bringing the spoon up close to the bowl and cutting down through again, around the bowl, until blended.

Frost. To cover with icing.

Fry. To fry in a pan in shortening or oil.

Grate. To reduce to small particles by rubbing against a grater.

Grind. To cut or crush with a food or nut grinder.

Hull. To remove the stem or hull of a fruit.

Knead. To work dough by pressing, folding, and stretching with the hands.

Mash. To mix or crush to a soft form.

Mix. To combine ingredients by stirring.

Pare or peel. To remove the outside skin.

Pit. To remove pits or seeds from fruit.

Puree. To push fruit or vegetables through a sieve.

Rinse. To wash lightly, usually with water.

Roast. To cook by dry heat, usually in an oven.

Roll. To place on a board and spread thin with a rolling pin.

Sauté. To cook or fry in a small amount of oil, shortening, or butter in a skillet.

Scald. To heat to temperature just below the boiling point until a skin forms on top.

Score. To cut narrow gashes part way through the outer surface.

Shred. To cut or tear into small slices or bits.

Shuck. To peel off the outer layer.

Sift. To pass through a sieve to remove lumps.

Simmer. To cook in liquid just below the boiling point.

Slice. To cut a thin, flat piece off.

Soak. To immerse in liquid.

Steam. To cook in steam that arises from a pan of boiling liquid.

Stir. To mix with a spoon.

Strain. To remove excess liquid, perhaps with a strainer or sieve.

Toss. To lightly mix ingredients.

Whip. To beat rapidly to incorporate air into the batter.

From *Cooking Up U.S. History*, Second Edition. © 1999 Suzanne I. Barchers and Patricia C. Marden. Teacher Ideas Press. (800) 237-6124.

Index of Recipes

About the Authors

Suzanne I. Barchers

Patricia C. Marden

Suzanne I. Barchers received her bachelor of science degree in elementary education from Eastern Illinois University, her master's degree in education in reading from Oregon State University, and her doctor of education degree in curriculum and instruction from the University of Colorado, Boulder.

After 15 years as a teacher and administrator in public and private schools, Suzanne began a writing and editing career. She has published more than 15 books, including college textbooks and the award-winning *Wise Women: Folk and Fairy Tales from Around the World* (Libraries Unlimited). She also co-authored *Cooking Up World History* (Teacher Ideas Press, 1994).

Suzanne has two adult sons and currently resides in Arvada, Colorado, with her husband, Dan. She teaches children's literature at the University of Colorado, Denver, and continues her writing and editing career.

Patricia Marden received her bachelor's degree in elementary education and her master's degree in reading at the University of Delaware. She was a primary school teacher and administrator in Hockessin, Delaware, for 10 years before moving to Colorado in 1982.

Patricia has worked in both independent and public schools for more than 25 years. She has received several government grants in the areas of experiential science, real-life math experiences, social studies, language arts, animals in the classroom, and computers in education. She has been involved in many professional groups including reading, writing, math, science, social studies, cooperative groupings, and multi-age groupings. She has also worked closely with Dr. Todd Siler (*How to Think Like a Genius*) and is currently involved in pilot programs using his "Artscience" methodology. Patricia received the Milken National Educator Award in 1991 and remains active in the organization.

Patricia resides in Littleton, Colorado, with her husband, Chris, and Great Pyrenees dog, Bozworth. She enjoys spending time with her granddaughter. She teaches in the Cherry Creek School District and enjoys using integrated themes, cooking, and children's literature to motivate children. She also co-authored *Cooking Up World History* (Teacher Ideas Press, 1994).